Second

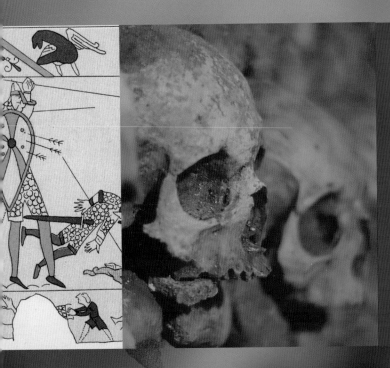

Invasion, Plague and Murder

Britain
1066–1485

Aaron Wilkes

James Ball

OXFORD
UNIVERSITY PRESS

OXFORD
UNIVERSITY PRESS

Great Clarendon Street, Oxford OX2 6DP

Oxford University Press is a department of the University of Oxford.
It furthers the University's objective of excellence in research,
scholarship,and education by publishing worldwide in

Oxford   New York

Auckland   Cape Town   Dar es Salaam   Hong Kong   Karachi
Kuala Lumpur   Madrid   Melbourne   Mexico City   Nairobi
New Delhi   Shanghai   Taipei   Toronto

With offices in

Argentina   Austria   Brazil   Chile   Czech Republic   France   Greece
Guatemala   Hungary   Italy   Japan   Poland   Portugal   Singapore
South Korea   Switzerland   Thailand   Turkey   Ukraine   Vietnam

Oxford is a registered trade mark of Oxford University Press
in the UK and in certain other countries

British Library Cataloguing in Publication Data

Data available

ISBN 978-1-85008-344-3

FD3443

10 9 8 7 6 5 4 3

Printed in China by Printplus

Paper used in the production of this book is a natural, recyclable product
made from wood grown in sustainable forests. The manufacturing process
conforms to the environmental regulations of the country of origin.

Editors: Daniel Bottom and Joanne Mitchell
Layout artist: Sally Boothroyd
Illustrations: Jamil Dar and Tony Randell
Cover design: Mike Cryer at EMC Design
Cover image: iStockphoto, Mary Evans Picture Library and Science Photo
Library

Acknowledgements

AA World Travel Library/TopFoto: pp39 (middle), pp47
Adam Woolfitt/Corbis: pp51 (top)
AFP/Getty Images: pp71
AKG Images: pp121, 122 (top)
Ancient Art and Architecture Collection Ltd: pp25, 107
Angelo Hornak/Corbis: pp136
Archives de l'Assistance Publique: pp53
Archivo Iconografico, S.A/Corbis: pp116
Bettman/Corbis: pp51 (bottom), 122 (bottom), 126-7
Bodiam Castle: pp57
Bodleian Library, Oxford: pp89
Bridgeman Art Library: pp8, 64, 89, 96, 97(top)
British Library: pp33, 79, 89 (right), 106 (bottom), 126, 127, 152
British Museum: pp10
CDC/PHIL/Corbis: p122 (middle)
Classical Numismatic Group, Inc: pp10 (left)
Claudia Dewald/iStockphoto: pp92
Clive Streeter/Dorling Kindersley: pp59 (bottom)
Corbis/Sygma: pp137
David Appleby/Twentieth Century/Bureau L.A. Collection/Corbis:
pp97 (bottom)
David G Britton/FreeFoto: pp135 (middle top & right, bottom left,)
Dorling Kindersley: Kim Sayer pp11
Fortean Picture Library: pp88
Fotolia/Mark Bond: pp41
Fotolia/Richard McGuirk: pp80
iStockphoto: pp7 (middle), 92, 135 (top left)
Ivan Volovin/JAI/Corbis: pp95 (bottom)
Joanne Mitchell: pp139
John Springer Collection/Corbis: pp151
London Aerial Photo Library, Ian/London Aerial Photo Library/Corbis:
pp106(top)
Lulu.com: pp99
Mary Evans Picture Library: pp26, 70, 73, 85, 89 (bottom), 101, 125
Michael Holford: pp22, 34
Michael Owen/iStockphoto: pp135 (lower right)
National Portrait Gallery, London: pp145
Nik Wheeler/Corbis: pp149
Private collection, Ken Welsh/Bridgeman: pp143
Ronald Sheridan/Ancient Art and Architecture Collection: pp59
Royal Collection Enterprises Limited: pp111
Royal Holloway, University of London/The Bridgeman Art Library:
pp142
Sandra Cunningham/Fotolia: pp117
Sonia Halliday Photographs: pp49, 95 (top)
Spanish School: pp9
Steven Vidler/Eurasia Press/Corbis: pp29
Terry J Alcorn/iStockphoto: pp92
The National Archives: pp31
TopFoto: Woodmansterne pp7 (bottom), pp39 (bottom)

Contents

What is history?

Before you start this book, take a few minutes to think about these questions.

- What do you think history is? What does the word mean?
- What have you learnt in history lessons before, perhaps in your primary school? Did you enjoy the lessons or not? If you didn't enjoy them, why not?
- Have you read any history books or stories about things that happened a long time ago? Have you watched any television programmes, films or plays about things that happened in the past? If so, which ones?

History is about what happened in the past. It is about people in the past, what they did and why they did it, what they thought and what they felt. To enjoy history you need to have a good imagination. You need to be able to imagine what life was like in the past, or what it may have been like to be involved in past events.

How did people feel, think and react to events like these?

It's a lovely summer's day. A festival has been organised in the local town. What games will I see – shin hacking, bear baiting, stoolball or coolhand? Will I join in with any of them?

A foreign army has invaded. I am part of an army that is marching to fight them. I must win the battle... or die! How big is their army? Is my axe sharp enough? Am I scared or not?

A deadly disease has arrived in my town. There's no cure. The family next door are all dead. Will I be next? What can I do to avoid it?

So what topics are in this book?

The subject of history doesn't just get you to use your imagination, it fills your mind with fascinating questions. Some of the fantastic facts you'll learn in this book will amaze you; others will leave you hungry for more… and some might even leave you reaching for the sick bucket! For example, there is information in this book which helps you discover:

- Why did a teenage nun fake her own death?

- Which king died after his bladder burst open?

- Whose brains were kicked around a cathedral floor?

- What disgusting job did a gong farmer do?

- Why was football banned in 1331?

History shows us how, why and when things have changed. At one time the king ruled all on his own. He could do what he wanted. He might ask his supporters, barons or earls for some help now and again, but ordinary people had no power at all. The king made the laws and everyone had to do what he said.

A few people were very rich, but most were very poor. The poor lived a hard life – if they got sick, they usually died. If they didn't work hard on their land, they usually starved. Few people cared.

Times have changed a lot since the Middle Ages. Today we have parliament, elections, law courts, hospitals and education for all. We have a queen, but she has very little real power compared with the kings and queens of the Middle Ages.

If we want to understand the world around us today, it's important that we know how it came to be this way.

Work ⌒.

Why not try to answer the questions at the top of page 4? You might discuss your answers with your classmates and/or your teacher before writing them down.

How to use this book

As you work through this book, you will notice a number of features that keep appearing:

—— MISSION OBJECTIVES ——

All sections of this book will start by setting your Mission Objectives. These are your key aims that set out your learning targets for the work ahead. Topics will end by trying to get you to assess your own learning. If you can accomplish each Mission Objective then you are doing well!

—— MISSION ACCOMPLISHED? ——

WISE-UP Words are key terms that are vital to help you discuss and understand the topics. You can spot them easily because they are in bold red type. Look up their meanings in a dictionary or use the Glossary at the end of the book. The Glossary is a list of these words with their meanings.

Some topics contain PAUSE for Thought boxes. This is an opportunity for you to stop and think for yourself.

The Hungry for MORE features give you a chance to extend your knowledge and research beyond the classroom. This is a time for you to take responsibility for your own learning. You might be asked to research something in the library or on the Internet, work on a presentation, or design and make something. Can you meet the challenge?

 FACT

These are all the fascinating, amazing or astounding little bits of history that you usually don't get to hear about! But in Folens History we think they are just as important and give you insights into topics that you'll easily remember.

HISTORICAL ENQUIRY

Historical Enquiries

There are also six Historical Enquiries in this book. These will get you to focus on the following themes:

- **HOW RELIGIOUS WERE PEOPLE IN THE MIDDLE AGES?**
- **HOW TOLERANT WERE PEOPLE IN THE MIDDLE AGES?**
- **WHO RULES?**
- **COULD YOU GET JUSTICE IN THE MIDDLE AGES?**
- **ENGLAND AT WAR**
- **ENGLAND ABROAD**

These themes will give you a broad knowledge of medieval religion, social attitudes and rules, power and England's relations with other countries.

Work sections are your opportunity to demonstrate your knowledge and understanding. You might be asked to put events in the correct chronological order. You might be asked to:

- explain how things have damaged over time;
- work out why two people might interpret the same event differently;
- work out what triggered an event to take place in the short term or the long term.

And finally...

This book will ask you to think. You will be asked to look at pieces of evidence to try to work things out for yourself. Sometimes two pieces of evidence about the same event won't agree with each other. You might be asked to think of reasons why. Your answers might not be the same as your friends' or even your teacher's answers. The important thing is to give reasons for your thoughts and answers. For example, think about the questions we are asking about each of these illustrations...

SOURCE A: *A modern artist has created this as a picture of what is known as a motte and bailey castle. These were the first types of castle that existed in this country. But why have we had to draw a picture of this? Why couldn't we have used a photo?* ↳

SOURCE B: *This is another one of the castles you'll study in the book. Note how castle design has changed. Why have we been able to include a photo of it in the book?* ↱

↳ **SOURCE C:** *Can you believe that this castle was also built during the period studied in this book! Note how different it looks. What factors could have caused these changes?*

England before 1066: What was it like?

MISSION OBJECTIVES

- How did England get its name?
- What was eleventh century England like?
- Who ruled England in the years up to 1066?

Imagine this:

• A foreign army invades England. The invaders kill the English King – and replace him with their own king. Most English people with important jobs have their jobs taken by the invaders and land is taken from the English people who own it – and given to the friends of the new king. The new rulers treat the English like slaves and punish them if they object or don't follow the new rules. Most old English buildings are pulled down and replaced by new ones built by the invaders and finally the invaders introduce a new language.

Surely this could never happen! Surely this has never happened! Well it did, in 1066 when an army from Normandy, an area in northern France, invaded England. All of these things listed above didn't happen straight away, but they definitely happened within a few years. Indeed, after 1066, England was never the same again.

But in order to understand just how amazing the dangers were, and the dramatic impact they had on England, we first need to look at what England was like before 1066.

↰ SOURCE A: *Edward the Confessor, King of England from 1042–66.*

Who rules?

The Romans ruled England up to about 410. From the year 800 onwards, **Vikings** from Denmark and Sweden invaded… … and many stayed. The Vikings lived mainly in the North and East of England, while the Anglo Saxons lived in the West and the South. The two sides fought each other for many years but had started to live well alongside each other by the eleventh century. Then tribes from northern Europe (now Germany, Denmark and Holland) called Angles, Saxons and Jutes invaded and stayed here. The climate was better and the land was less marshy than their own! The Britons were slowly pushed into Wales and what is now Cornwall by the invaders. Some even left their homeland altogether and settled in the part of France we now call Brittany. Meanwhile the Scots (an Irish tribe), began to settle in what we now call Scotland. They fought with the Picts, who already lived there. Eventually the two tribes joined, but the Scots gave their name to the country.

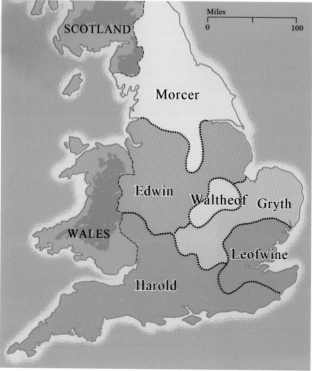

↵ SOURCE B: *Earldoms.*

★WISE-UP Words

Anglo-Saxons earl
earldom evidence Vikings

Although there seems to have been more Saxon tribesmen than Angles or Jutes, the country we now call England gradually became known as Angleland. And the people who lived there were known as **Anglo-Saxons**. Some called them 'the English'.

In 1065 Edward the Confessor ruled England, and was helped in his new role by lots of different people. Some were Englishmen from rich, important families who looked after an area of England called an **earldom** (see Source B). But King Edward also took advice from some of the Norman friends he brought over from Normandy. This led to tension between the English and the Normans. The king even spoke Norman French better than he spoke English!

So how many people were there?

The population of the whole of England was about 1.5 million people. Nearly everybody worked as farmers on the land that had been cleared. Much of England was still covered by forests. People lived in small villages and probably spent most of their lives there. There were few towns – only about 15 with more than 1000 people living there. And only eight towns had a population of more than 3000 (see Source C).

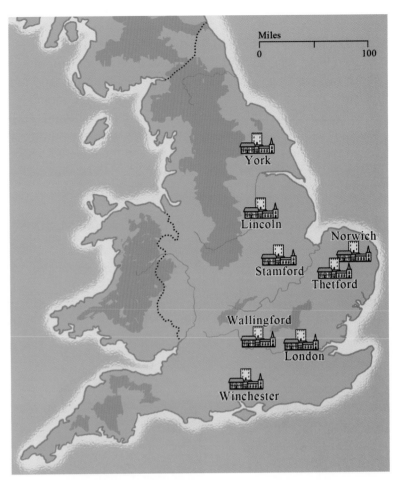

↥ SOURCE C: *The eight largest towns in 1066.*

SOURCE D: *England's farmers were some of the best in Europe.*

'The English wore short garments, reaching to the knees. They had short hair, their beards shaven; their arms covered with gold bracelets; their skin covered with pictured designs. Drinking parties were common and they drank until they were sick. Drunkenness weakens the human mind and they often fought with fury rather than with military skill.'

↥ SOURCE E: *A description of the English by a monk in 1130.*

How rich was England?

The rich were very rich and the poor were very poor. Out of every 100 people, about two were rich. They made their money from the land they owned (because people paid them rent to live on it) or from trading in leather, iron or wool. Some men made so much money they built fabulous homes and churches and lived in luxury. By contrast, life was very hard for the poor. Each family had to grow its own food – and there were no shops like today where we can buy more if we run out. If the harvest was bad, a family might have to eat roots, leaves, wild berries and any creatures they could catch. People often died of small wounds and infections because there were no medicines except herbs.

> **! FACT** Kerrrrching!!
> The currency was pounds (£), shillings (s) and pence (d). There were 12d in a shilling and 20s in a pound. A farm worker would earn about 1d a day, enough to buy basic food and supplies.

SOURCE E: *Anglo-Saxon coins. The money system used in 1066 was still being used in England up to 1974.*

SOURCE F: *The Alfred Jewel, which was made of gold and precious stones. Around the edge it reads 'Alfred had me made.' Alfred was an Anglo-Saxon king from 871–901. A long stick fitted into the hole at the bottom. The whole thing then became a pointer for following words in a book.*

Were people religious?

The simple answer is 'yes'. Everyone was a Christian and went to church. In monasteries (large buildings where monks lived) monks kept huge official diaries called chronicles. They wrote about religion, politics, history, towns, kings, gossip and even the weather.

SOURCE G: *A page from a monk's chronicle.*

How do we know all this?

We certainly don't know everything about England in 1066. However we know enough to give us a good idea about what life was like. We can look at a number of different sources from Anglo-Saxon times, which allow us to build up a picture of their lives – paintings, churches and other buildings, coins, weapons, drawings, jewellery and books. These sources are **evidence** of life in England in 1066.

↳ **SOURCE H:** *The Anglo-Saxon church of St Lawrence at Bradford on Avon, Wiltshire. As you can see, the church is very strong and may have been used as a fortress in times of trouble.*

Work

1 Some written sources in this book were written by chroniclers. These were men who wrote chronicles from their own point of view. They wrote about what they believed and felt, rather than what they actually saw. Why is it important to know this when studying history?

2 Use pages 8-11 to write your own fact file about England in 1066. You should use ten sentences to write ten different facts. Add the title "My top ten facts about England in 1066."

3 The beginnings and endings of these sentences have been mixed up. Using the information on these two pages, match up the start of the sentences (List A) with the correct ending (List B).

LIST A	LIST B
Romans, Anglo-Saxons and Vikings	was about 1.5 million
London	were some of the best in Europe
England's farmers	have all invaded England at one time or another
Edward the Confessor	was England's largest town in 1066
The population of England in 1066	was King of England in 1066

--- **MISSION ACCOMPLISHED?** ---

• Can you explain the difference between an earl and an earldom… … and explain what is meant by the term 'Anglo-Saxon'?

Who will be the next King of England?

MISSION OBJECTIVES

- Why did three different men claim to be King of England in 1066?
- Who were the three contenders and who had the best claim to the throne?

1066 is probably the most famous year in British history. Many of you will have heard of it even though you haven't studied it yet. 1066 is so well known because it was the last time England was invaded and taken over by a foreign power. The English King and his followers were killed and the country was divided up between the new invaders. England's language, rulers and way of life changed forever. What a year!

The old king Dies...

In January 1066, Edward the Confessor, King of England, died. He was 62 years old and left no children behind. There was no clear **heir** to the throne. However, three men believed that they should be England's next King – and they were ready to use their armies to get their hands on the crown!

THE NORMAN

Name: William of Normandy

Position: Duke of Normandy, the strongest part of France.

Family history: William came from a fighting family. He had been in control of Normandy since he was seven and was used to having to fight to keep his lands.

Links to King Edward: Edward had lived in Normandy from 1016–1042. When Edward returned to England to be king, William sent soldiers to help him. As a result, King Edward had promised William the throne in 1051.

Was he tough enough? His nickname was 'William the Bastard' because his father wasn't married to his mother. In 1047, people from the town of Alençon made fun of his mother's family. William captured the town and ordered that 30 of the townsmen be skinned alive.

Support for his claim: According to William of Poitiers, a Norman writer, 'Edward, king of the English, loved William like a brother or son... so he decided that William should be the next king.' Harold Godwinson had visited William to tell him this news in 1064 and promised to support William's claim to the English crown.

THE ENGLISHMAN

Name: Harold Godwinson

Position: Earl of Wessex, one of the most powerful men in England.

Family history: His father, Godwin, argued a lot with King Edward. At one time Harold and his father were banished from England, but they returned a year later.

Links to King Edward: Harold's sister was married to King Edward.

Was he tough enough? Harold was a brave and respected soldier with a tough streak. In 1063, King Edward sent Harold to crush a Welsh uprising. The Welsh leader was caught and his head was chopped off on Harold's orders.

Support for his claim: He was the only Englishman claiming the throne. The Witan, a meeting of the most important bishops and earls in England, wanted Harold to be the next king. English monks wrote: 'Harold and his brothers were the king's favourites... on his deathbed that wise king promised the kingdom to Harold.'

The Englishman's advantage

When King Edward died on 5th January 1066, Harold had one big advantage over his two rivals. William and Hardrada were miles away across the sea while Harold was sitting pretty in England. He wasted no time and was crowned King the very next day – but he knew that wasn't the end of it. The other two would soon hear the news and come looking for him – and they'd both want him dead!

THE VIKING

Name: Harald Hardrada

Position: King of Norway.

Family history: He had fought alongside several Norwegian kings and had taken part in raids on the English coast. When he became King of Norway, he began to plan a full-scale invasion of England.

Links to King Edward: None – but a Viking called Canute had ruled Norway and England from 1016-1035.

Was he tough enough? He was the most feared warrior in Europe – tough, bloodthirsty and he enjoyed watching his enemies suffer. Hardrada means 'hard ruler' and his nickname was 'the Ruthless'.

Support for his claim: Harald's claim was supported by Tostig, Harold Godwinson's brother. The two brothers had fallen out and Tostig wanted revenge.

Hardrada and his men were from Norway. People from this area were known as Vikings.

NORWAY

Harold was English and his followers were Englishmen. England at this time sometimes called Saxon England and the people were called Anglo-Saxons.

ENGLAND

Wessex

FRANCE

Normandy

William and his men came from a part of France called Normandy. They were known as Normans.

WISE-UP Words

heir

Norman   Viking

Work

Now you have read about the three contenders for the throne, you must decide who you think had the best claim (reason to be king).

1 Copy and complete the following table. Try to include as many reasons as possible.

Contender	Why they should be king	Why they shouldn't be king
Harold Godwinson		
Harald Hardrada		
William of Normandy		

2 List the three contenders in the order that you think had the strongest claim. Label your first choice 'strongest' and your last choice 'weakest'.

3 In your own words, explain why you placed the three contenders in the order you have chosen.

— MISSION ACCOMPLISHED? —

- Can you explain why there was a disagreement over who was King of England in 1066?
- Could you tell someone about the three men who claimed the throne, why they thought it was theirs and who you think should have been king?

Round 1: The Battle of Stamford Bridge

—————— MISSION OBJECTIVES ——————
- Which of the contenders for the English throne fought at the battle of Stamford Bridge?
- Which of the contenders was favourite to win the crown after the battle?

For nine months, King Harold of England sat nervously on his throne, waiting for his rivals to make a move for his crown. In September 1066 his wait was over. Hardrada, King of Norway, had landed near York in the North of England and he wasn't leaving until the crown was his. With him was Harold's younger brother, Tostig. Oh, and about 10,000 bloodthirsty Vikings!

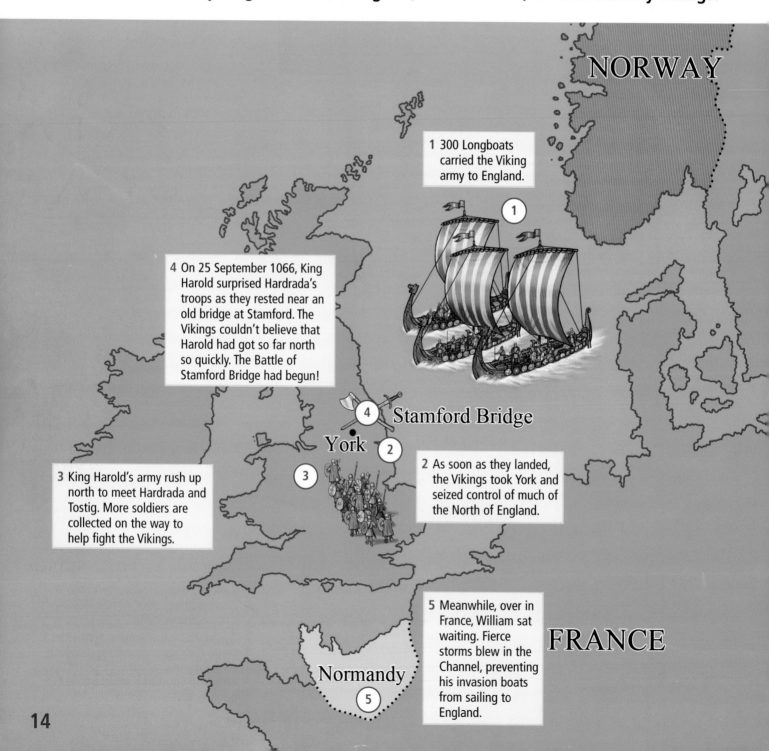

NORWAY

1 300 Longboats carried the Viking army to England.

4 On 25 September 1066, King Harold surprised Hardrada's troops as they rested near an old bridge at Stamford. The Vikings couldn't believe that Harold had got so far north so quickly. The Battle of Stamford Bridge had begun!

Stamford Bridge

York

2 As soon as they landed, the Vikings took York and seized control of much of the North of England.

3 King Harold's army rush up north to meet Hardrada and Tostig. More soldiers are collected on the way to help fight the Vikings.

5 Meanwhile, over in France, William sat waiting. Fierce storms blew in the Channel, preventing his invasion boats from sailing to England.

FRANCE

Normandy

1 It is early morning...

2 The battle starts badly for Hardrada's men. Some have left their armour several miles away.

3 Hardrada's men seem to be gaining control. One brave Viking blocks the bridge.

4 With no way over the bridge, Hardrada's army fight Harold's men to a standstill.

Wake up, wake up! King Harold is here!

STAMFORD BRIDGE

Where did you leave your chainmail?

Near the boats... sorry!

I've killed 40 Englishmen with my mighty axe!

5 After an hour, King Harold's men try to stop the warrior.

6 The Viking is killed and the English can get across the bridge.

7 By midday King Harold's army is in control. Hardrada is killed.

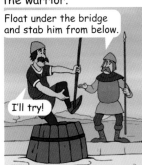

Float under the bridge and stab him from below.

I'll try!

Quick! Let's attack the Vikings while we have the chance!

Hurry – some have no armour.

Arghhh!

Our great King of Norway is dead!

8 Tostig is soon found and cut into pieces.

9 King Harold is the winner.

10 Out of respect, Harold buries his dead brother in York. But bad news arrives...

Kill him!

Cut him up!

They only need 24 ships to take their battered army home to Norway!

You'll have to fight again soon, my Lord. William of Normandy has landed near Hastings.

Earl Tostig

Work

1 The following statements are all reasons that explain why King Harold defeated Hardrada at the Battle of Stamford Bridge. Write these statements out in the correct chronological order.
- The Viking warrior blocking the bridge was killed.
- The few Vikings still alive escaped in 24 ships.
- Hardrada was killed.
- The Vikings didn't expect to see Harold's army so soon.
- Many of Hardrada's men did not have their armour.

2 a Write out the following statements, starting with the one that you think was most important in helping Harold win the Battle of Stamford Bridge.
- Hardrada was killed quite early in the battle.
- The Vikings were caught unprepared and without armour.
- The Viking blocking the bridge was killed.

Now, writing in full sentences and using capital letters and full stops, explain why you have put them in the order you have.

2 b Who do you believe is now favourite to become King of England? Who is definitely out of the contest? Again, writing in full sentences, explain your choices.

MISSION ACCOMPLISHED?
- Could you explain who was definitely not going to become King of England after the Battle of Stamford Bridge and why?
- Do you know who was left in the struggle for the English crown?
- Have you explained who you think will end up being King of England?

Match of the day!

MISSION OBJECTIVES

- What weapons and tactics were used by William's and Harold's men at the Battle of Hastings?

Harold's Housecarls

(CURRENT CHAMPIONS)

William's Knights

(THE CHALLENGERS)

⚽

DATE: 14 OCTOBER 1066
VENUE: SENLAC HILL, NEAR HASTINGS
· KICK OFF: 9.30 AM·

Hello and welcome to the town of Hastings. This is the one we've all been waiting over ten months for – the day of the battle is finally here. Here's the English line up. It's been a tough few weeks for the Saxon boys, despite last week's stunning victory at Stamford Bridge. The weary English have travelled 280 miles/ 450km in 17 days to meet their next opponents.

HOUSECARLS

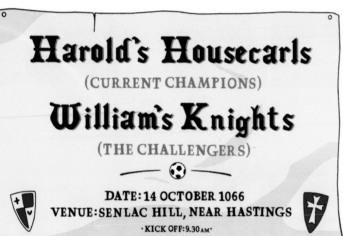

chain mail

battleaxe

KILLING POWER: 95

DEFENCE: 95

SPEED: 10

RANGE OF ATTACK: 5

The backbone of King Harold's army, there are about 2500 of them and they are well paid, fully trained and armed with the finest weapons. The favourite weapon of these bearded **warriors** is the huge **battleaxe**. The handle of the axe is over a metre long and its heavy blade is made of razor-sharp iron – a very precious material in 1066. A **housecarl** with a battleaxe is capable of chopping the head off a horse or cutting a man in half with a single blow. Their helmets, **chain mail**, large, round shields and discipline make them excellent in defence too!

THE FYRD

javelin

sword

shield

KILLING POWER: 30

DEFENCE: 45

SPEED: 15

RANGE OF ATTACK: 10

The housecarls are supported by the **fyrd**. This mobile army isn't as experienced or as well equipped as the housecarls but it's still a fierce fighting force. The leaders of the fyrd are armed with **swords** and **javelins** but most of their men use farming tools such as pitchforks and **scythes**. They may not be pretty, but they number over 6000 and they're fighting on their home turf!

Now let's have a look at the Normans. They've been waiting for this day ever since Harold was crowned in January and they're itching for a fight. William's invasion force is massive: it took over 300 ships to transport his 10 000 men and 2000 horses from France. He's even brought a flat-pack fort with him! They landed at Pevensey on 28 September and soon moved to Hastings, setting fire to the town to annoy Harold.

WISE-UP Words

archers battleaxe
chain mail fyrd
hauberks housecarl
invasion javelins
knights mace
scythes spears
swords warriors

NORMAN FOOT SOLDIERS

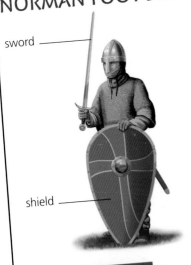

sword

shield

KILLING POWER: 50

DEFENCE: 50

SPEED: 15

RANGE OF ATTACK: 10

These form the main part of William's army and are armed with metre-long swords and kite-shaped shields. They attack after the enemy have been softened up by the archers' arrows and charges by the **knights**.

THE ARCHERS

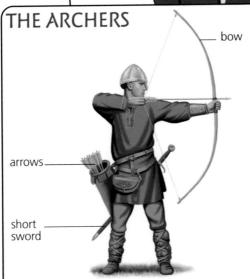

bow

arrows

short sword

KILLING POWER: 40

DEFENCE: 5

SPEED: 35

RANGE OF ATTACK: 99

William's 1500 **archers** are armed with small wooden bows that can fire six or seven arrows a minute. A skilled archer can kill a man from about 180m away. Archers have very little, if any, armour and are not much use when the fighting gets up close and personal!

THE KNIGHTS

hauberk

spear

warhorse

KILLING POWER: 80

DEFENCE: 40

SPEED: 95

RANGE OF ATTACK: 70

William's best warriors are his 2000 knights: highly trained and fiercely loyal professional soldiers. They ride into battle on big, strong, warhorses and are protected by metal helmets, chain mail suits (**hauberks**) and kite-shaped shields. Knights carry **spears** (which can be thrown or used to stab the enemy), a sword or a **mace** (a heavy metal club covered in spikes). Knights charge at full speed towards their opponents, hacking and slashing at the much slower soldiers fighting on foot beneath them.

Work

1 Match up the words on the left with the correct description on the right.

Housecarl Can fire six or seven arrows per minute.
Fyrd Mobile army of about 2000 Englishmen.
Archers Well trained and fully armed. They ride strong warhorses.
Knights Fought on foot. An important part of William's army.

2 Find two ways in which William's army is better than Harold's.

3 Find two ways in which Harold's army is better than William's.

4 Which army do you think is more likely to win the battle? Give reasons and answer in full sentences.

MISSION ACCOMPLISHED?

- Can you explain which weapons and tactics each side used?
- Could you tell the person next to you who you think would win in a battle and why?

Round 2: The Battle of Hastings – the morning

_____ MISSION OBJECTIVES _____
- What were the tactics used in the battle by Harold and William?
- Where and how did each of the armies fight in the early stages of the battle?

The final showdown had arrived. The Battle of Hastings would decide the future of England. King Harold had already defeated Hardrada and his Viking army and now, less than a month later, he and his army were going to have to fight all over again.

Unfortunately for Harold and his men, there had been no time to rest after Stamford Bridge – they had to march the 250 miles to meet William's men! So just where did the two armies line up to face each other? Who made the first move? And which side made the best start to the battle?

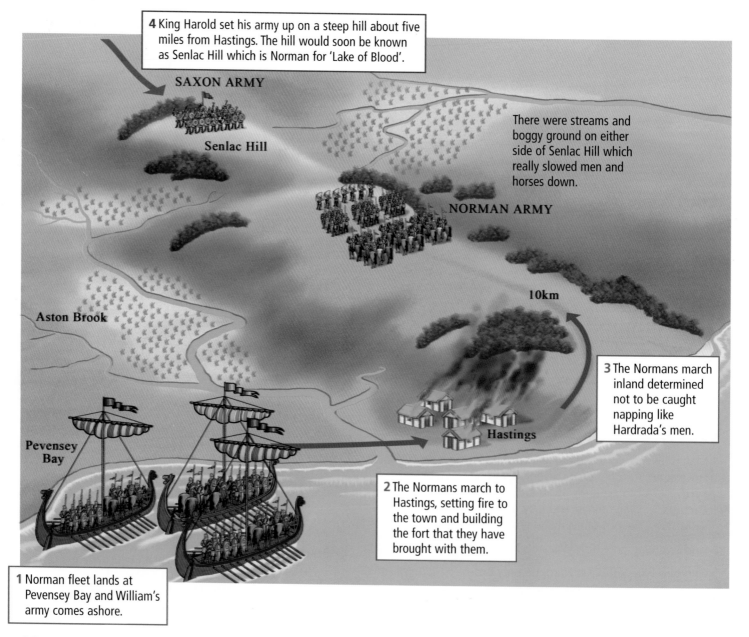

4 King Harold set his army up on a steep hill about five miles from Hastings. The hill would soon be known as Senlac Hill which is Norman for 'Lake of Blood'.

SAXON ARMY

Senlac Hill

There were streams and boggy ground on either side of Senlac Hill which really slowed men and horses down.

NORMAN ARMY

Aston Brook

10km

3 The Normans march inland determined not to be caught napping like Hardrada's men.

Hastings

Pevensey Bay

2 The Normans march to Hastings, setting fire to the town and building the fort that they have brought with them.

1 Norman fleet lands at Pevensey Bay and William's army comes ashore.

On 14 October, at around 9.30 in the morning, the Battle of Hastings began. William carried a flag given to him by the **Pope**. He believed this meant God was on his side. Looking up the steep hill to the English, William ordered his archers to unleash a storm of arrows.

Harold's men formed a tight **shield-wall** and hid behind it while the arrows fell amongst them. When the archers stopped firing, the English stood up and starting banging their shields and shouting, 'Out! Out! Out!'.

William decided to send his knights and foot soldiers to smash through the English shield-wall. Unfortunately for William, the steep hill meant his horses couldn't charge quickly. His foot soldiers were absolutely exhausted before they had even started fighting!

For over two hours the battle raged. The two sides stood toe-to-toe, hacking, slashing and stabbing viciously at each other. William's men just could not break through the wall of English shields that stretched across the hill-top. Then a rumour started to spread that nobody had seen William for half an hour! Had the Norman leader been killed?

William wasn't dead and to prove it to his men he galloped amongst them. He lifted his helmet and shouted, 'Look at me! Look at me! I am alive and, with God's help, will be the victor!'

Work

1 **Battle analysis** Divide your page into two and separate the following list into factors that would help Harold win the battle and factors that would help William win the battle.
   - William's army had been blessed by the Pope.
   - Harold's men had just come from a battle with Hardrada.
   - The housecarls protected Harold's army with a strong shield wall.
   - William had a large army of 10 000 men.
   - There were streams and boggy ground on both sides of Senlac Hill.

2 Write two sentences that explain why Harold placed his soldiers on the top of Senlac Hill.

3 Which side do you think is most likely to win the battle in the afternoon? Give reasons for your answer in full sentences.

★ WISE-UP Words

Pope
shield-wall

— MISSION ACCOMPLISHED? —

- Can you explain where Harold placed his army?
- Could you tell someone how William decided to attack the English army?
- Have you decided who you think is the favourite to win the battle in the afternoon?

Round 2: The Battle of Hastings – the afternoon

___ MISSION OBJECTIVES ___
- How did William win the Battle of Hastings?
- How did William go about increasing his power after the battle?

After a short break in the action, the battle started again at around 12.30pm. Neither side seemed to be winning and the same thing kept happening over and over again. The Normans kept attacking and the English kept beating away the attacks with their shield-wall. At around 3.30pm, William came up with an idea. So what was William's big plan? How was he going to get through that shield-wall? And what did this mean for King Harold?

William had to get the English off the top of the hill. He ordered some of his soldiers who were fighting to run away down the hill as if they were **retreating**. The English, thinking they were winning, charged down the hill after the Normans!

Without the safety of the shield-wall, Harold's men who had run down the hill were quickly cut to pieces by William's knights on horseback.

William saw this was his chance to win the battle – and the English crown! He hoped that if he kept repeating the trick, the English would keep falling for it. And they did! Gradually, the English shield-wall grew weaker and weaker. William then turned to his archers once more and arrows rained down on Harold's men.

At about 6.00pm, Harold was killed and the battle was lost. Harold's body was identified later in the evening but it was in a terrible state. Harold Godwinson, the King of England, had been **disembowelled**! William had the body buried at a secret location despite Harold's mother offering her son's weight in gold in exchange for the body.

After the battle

On the night of the 14 October 1066, the Normans held a feast to celebrate their victory and stripped the English dead of their weapons and armour. He may have defeated Harold's army, but William only ruled as far as he could see. Early the next morning, William left Senlac Hill and marched towards London. He made sure that every town he came across surrendered to him, while more and more soldiers sailed from Normandy to join him. By early December, William had reached London and he was crowned King of England on Christmas Day. From now on he was known as William the **Conqueror**!

The enemy within!

Although there was no danger of William being defeated by an army after Hastings, he was very nearly defeated by **dysentery**. While on the road to London, William's army was struck by agonising stomach cramps and violent diarrhoea. For some it was so bad that they had to return home to France – others died! Fortunately for William, enough remained fit to continue to London.

'Three horses were killed under him. Three times he leapt unafraid to the ground and killed the man who had killed his horse. This shows how quick he was to make his mind up and how strong he was. With savage blows of his sword, he split shields, helmets and coats of chain mail. He struck a number of enemies with his own shield. His soldiers took new courage when they saw him fighting on foot. Some, who were weak from bleeding, leant on their shields and fought on bravely. William himself helped some of his men to safety.'

SOURCE A: *Taken from a history textbook from the 1980s.*

"
He led his forces with great skill, holding them when they turned to run, giving them courage, sharing their danger. He was more often heard shouting to them to follow him than ordering them to go on ahead. It is clear that it was the Duke's bravery that inspired his soldiers as they went forward and gave them courage.
"

SOURCE B: *An account of William fighting in the battle, written in 1073.*

WISE-UP Words

conqueror
disembowelled
dysentery
retreating

Work

1 Read Sources A and B. Write down five adjectives or phrases that describe William in battle.

2 **Chronology task!** Read back through the story of the battle. Create a time line for the battle, starting at 9.30am in the morning. Remember to include all the key events and the time they happened.

3 Why do you think the Normans stripped the English of all their weapons and armour? How could this help William control the rest of England? Answer in full sentences and use capital letters and full stops.

4 You should now know what happened at the Battle of Hastings. It's time to make up your mind – why did William win the battle? Was it:
- because he was a brilliant and skilful leader?
- because Harold was a poor soldier who made mistakes?
- because the Normans were better equipped and prepared?
- because Harold was unlucky?

Or was it a combination of all or some of these reasons?

MISSION ACCOMPLISHED?

- Do you know how William finally managed to break the English shield-wall?
- Could you explain to somebody what happened to King Harold?
- Do you know how William began to control the rest of England and do you know what problems he faced?

How did King Harold die?

• How did King Harold of England die at the Battle of Hastings?

Look at the picture below very carefully. One of the most famous in British history, it is one of 70 pictures which make up a 70 metre long piece of embroidered cloth called the Bayeux Tapestry. The tapestry was made in 1077 in Bayeux, Normandy (where it is kept today) by local women on the orders of Bishop Odo, King William's half-brother. Odo was at the Battle of Hastings.

SOURCE A: *A section from the Bayeux Tapestry – but which soldier is King Harold? And look carefully along the bottom of the tapestry to see what the Norman soldiers did to the English dead after the defeat.* ⤵

The scene shows two English soldiers, one with an arrow in his eye and another being cut down by a Norman soldier on horseback. Above the picture is written 'Harold Rex Interfectus est' which means 'here King Harold dies'. But which one is meant to be Harold? Is it the one on the left pulling an arrow from his eye or the one on the right being chopped down with a sword?

How King Harold died is one of the biggest mysteries of the Battle of Hastings. We definitely know he died because a new King of England began ruling England, but we don't know exactly how he died!

EVIDENCE A
Date: 1068
Writer: A Norman monk, name unknown.

"With the point of his **lance** the first knight pierced Harold's shield and chest, drenching the ground with blood. With his sword the second knight cut off his head. The third disembowelled him with his javelin. The fourth hacked off his leg."

EVIDENCE B
Date: 1070–71
Writer: William of Jumieges, a Norman monk. He claims he was at the battle. His **abbey** was given money by William the Conqueror.

"Duke William engaged the enemy at the third hour [about 9am] and continued until nightfall. Harold fell in the first shock of the battle, pierced with lethal wounds."

EVIDENCE C
Date: 1125
Writer: William of Malmesbury, a monk. Historians believe this source was written after he had seen the Bayeux Tapestry.

"Harold continued; but when he fell, from having his brain pierced with an arrow... he yielded to death... one of the soldiers with a sword gashed his thigh as he lay."

EVIDENCE D
Date: 2000
Writer: Simon Schama, a modern historian who presents history programmes for the BBC.

"How did Harold himself die? Lately there's been an attempt to read the death scene in the Bayeux Tapestry as though he was the figure cut down by the horsemen, not the warrior pulling the arrow out of his eye... but it seems to me perfectly clear that the words 'Harold Rex' occur directly and significantly above the arrow-struck figure... then certainly the knights would have been on him."

WISE-UP Words

abbey
lance

'Then it was that an arrow which was that towards the sky struck Harold above the right eye and that one of his eyes it put out.'

EVIDENCE E: *Written in 1067 by Guy of Amiens, a medieval writer.*

Historians (people who study history – like you) know lots about the year 1066. Some people wrote about it at the time; others told stories about it (which were then written down) and some people made pictures showing it.

The problem with King Harold's death is that the sources (pieces of evidence) don't always agree about what happened. Your task is to treat his death as a mystery. Look through the evidence and come to your own conclusion on this key question: 'How did King Harold die?'.

Work

To try to solve the mystery of how Harold died, start by looking closely at all the evidence on this page.

1 **Find out all the different ways Harold may have died.**
   What weapons were used? At what stage of the battle did he die? Make a list of your findings.

2 **Find out if any of the evidence agrees on how Harold was killed.**
   Does any one piece of evidence back up what another says? Write down notes on what you have found.

3 **Think – can you trust the evidence?**
   Write down why you might not trust some of the evidence. You may believe all the evidence is useful or perhaps just some of it. Do we have an English eyewitness to Harold's death? If not, why not?

4 **Now make your decision.**
   Like a detective, use evidence to back up your theory. If you're not sure, say why. In history it's OK to say you're uncertain, as long as you can explain why.

! FACT **How do opinions differ?!!**
There are some things that we just don't know about the past. Some historians say the evidence proves how Harold was killed. Others say it proves we can't be sure. These disagreements are one of the things that make history so fascinating.

—— MISSION ACCOMPLISHED? ——

• Could you write down, in no more than 50 words, how you think Harold died and explain how you arrived at your conclusion?

The conquest of England

MISSION OBJECTIVES

• To understand William's key problems when he became King of England and how he dealt with them.

On the evening of 14 October 1066 (the night of the Battle of Hastings), William must have realised he was in a very dangerous position. As a foreign invader, he knew the English would want to get rid of him – soon! His army had killed the English King Harold after all, and William knew that if he gave the English time to recover they might gather another army or choose another king. So how did William deal with these problems?

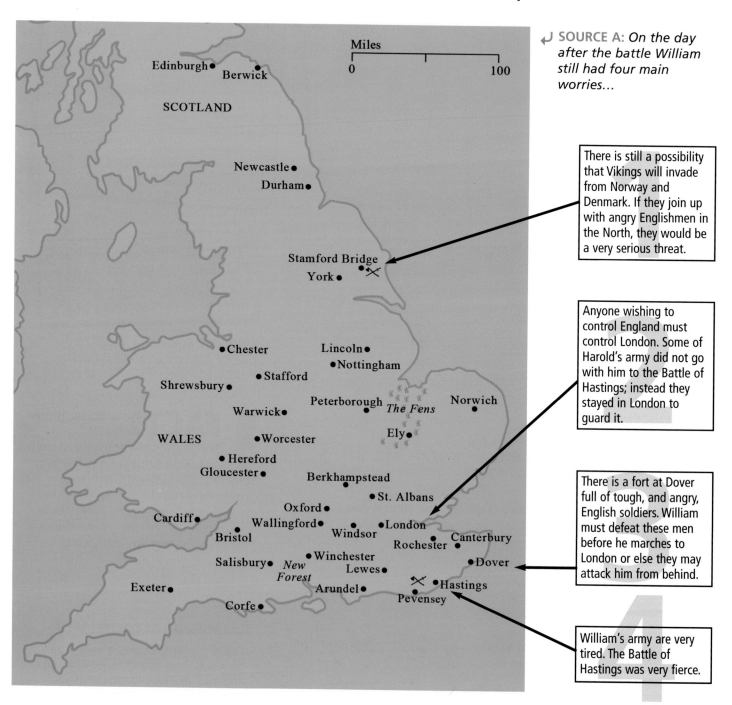

↵ SOURCE A: *On the day after the battle William still had four main worries...*

1 There is still a possibility that Vikings will invade from Norway and Denmark. If they join up with angry Englishmen in the North, they would be a very serious threat.

2 Anyone wishing to control England must control London. Some of Harold's army did not go with him to the Battle of Hastings; instead they stayed in London to guard it.

3 There is a fort at Dover full of tough, and angry, English soldiers. William must defeat these men before he marches to London or else they may attack him from behind.

4 William's army are very tired. The Battle of Hastings was very fierce.

Source A shows you some of William's immediate problems, and one of his solutions. Sources B, C and D were written or embroidered at the time and show how determined William was to keep his new kingdom … and show the English who was boss.

"

William marched to Dover where the English, stricken with fear, prepared to surrender. But our men, greedy for loot, set fire to the castle. William, unwilling that those who had offered to give up, should suffer loss, gave them money for the damage his men had caused. Having captured the castle William spent eight days making it stronger.

"

↰ **SOURCE B:** *Written by William of Poitiers in about 1071.*

'The Archbishop of York, the people of London and some powerful English landowners planned to put Prince Edgar (a cousin of King Edward the Confessor) on the throne. But while many were preparing to fight the powerful English landowners with their army, William was robbing and destroying villages in Sussex, Kent, Hampshire, Middlesex and Hertfordshire. He was even slaughtering people in these villages. William was then met by the English landowners and the leading men of London who agreed to accept him as King.'

↰ **SOURCE C:** *Florence of Worcester describes William's movements before he went to London.*

SOURCE D: *The Bayeux Tapestry showing the Normans burning an English house.* ↴

Work ⁓.

1 In your own words, explain what problems King William faced immediately after the Battle of Hastings.

2 Look at Sources B, C and D.

   a Why do you think William was kind to the English in Dover but so cruel as he marched towards London?

   b In what way is Source C similar to Source D?

25

ENGLAND UNDER THE NORMANS

William took two months to reach London, and on the way his army burnt, stole and killed anything it passed. In December, the English soldiers in London gave in and William entered the city. He was crowned King of England in Westminster Abbey on Christmas Day 1066 (see Source E).

But the new king still had to conquer the rest of England. And the people in the North of England, helped by Vikings from Denmark, weren't giving up easily. When William's trusted friend, Earl Robert, and 900 of William's soldiers were murdered when they were sent up to rule Durham, the king acted quickly – and brutally – to deal with the rebels. Sources F, G and H show just how tough the new king was.

⤺ **SOURCE E:** *William crowned King of England, from the Bayeux Tapestry.*

'William gave Northumberland to Earl Robert (his friend) but the people of Durham **massacred** Robert and 900 of his soldiers. Prince Edgar and the rebels came to York and the people of the city joined them. William came from the south and surprised them, ravaging York and killing hundreds. Then Vikings came from Denmark with 240 ships and joined up with the English. With a huge and joyful army they stormed York and killed hundreds of William's men, burned the castle and captured lots of treasure.'

⤺ **SOURCE F:** *Rebellion in the North from the 'Anglo-Saxon Chronicle'.*

'William came to York but learned that the Vikings had fled. He ordered his men to repair the castle. He set out to search the forests and remote mountains, stopping at nothing to hunt down the rebels hidden there. He cut down many and destroyed and burned homes. Nowhere else had William shown such cruelty. His fury was blind and he punished the innocent with the guilty. He ordered that all crops, cattle and food be burned, so that the whole region had nothing to live on.'

⤺ **SOURCE G:** *William's revenge known as the 'Harrying of the North' was brutal. Some estimate that 100 000 people died from starvation after William's troops had destroyed all the animals and crops.*

'I fell on the Northern shires like a hungry lion. I ordered their houses and corn with all their tools and goods to be burnt and great herds of cattle to be butchered. I took my revenge by giving them famine. Alas I kept the throne by so many crimes.'

⤺ **SOURCE H:** *King William's deathbed confession, written by Oderic Vitalis in about 1130. Oderic wasn't there and has given his own opinion on what William said.*

King William's men built castles to control the areas they conquered. Source I shows the spread of his castle-making plans in the years after Hastings. And he brought over dozens of his most loyal friends from Normandy to live in them. By 1071, five years after he had won the Battle of Hastings, King William was master of England – William the Conqueror. His next challenge was to stay in charge!

WISE-UP Words

massacred

SOURCE I: *The Norman Conquest, 1066–1070. William's castle-building spread across the country.*

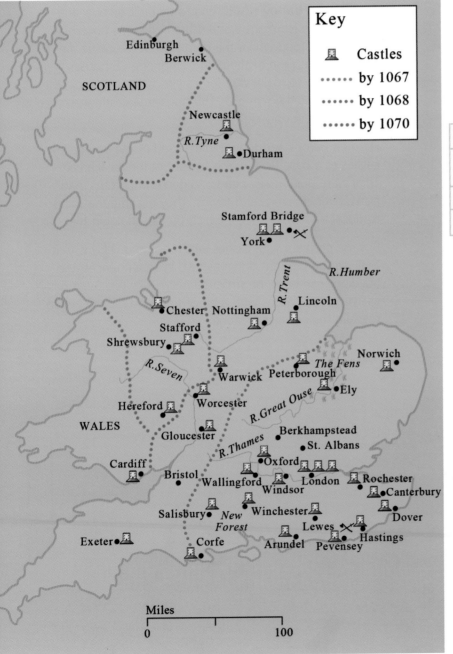

Key

🏰   Castles

•••••• by 1067

•••••• by 1068

•••••• by 1070

Work

1 The way King William crushes the North of England is known as the 'Harrying of the North'. Copy and complete the following table. You will find the information in the text and sources.

The Harrying of the North	1068–1070
Causes of rebellion in the North	
English actions	
William's actions	

2 Look at Source G.
  a How did William use famine as a weapon?
  b What are the advantages and disadvantages of this?

3 Historians have said that William punished the people in the North to teach the whole country a lesson. Explain what this means.

MISSION ACCOMPLISHED?

- Can you explain how King William dealt with some of the immediate problems he faced in 1066?

How did King William keep control of England?

—————————————— MISSION OBJECTIVES ——————————————
- To understand how King William used castles, barons and a book to control his new kingdom.

To the English, King William was a foreigner. He was a Frenchman, who spoke French and had French friends. Most Englishmen hated him and wanted him dead! But after about five years as king, William had managed to put down all the rebellions against his rule. He now had to think about the long-term future. How could he stay in control of England? Who might help him run the country? And just how much was England worth?

William builds castles

William brought his rich and powerful friends over from Normandy to help control the English. In return for this support he gave them large areas of English land. These friends became powerful landowners known as barons. Men soon realised that they needed protection from attacks by unhappy Englishmen. So they decided to build castles. And, by 1086, King William's barons had built over 100 castles across England (see Source B).

Reduced to rubble

Motte and bailey castles had to be built quickly, and wherever the Normans wanted them. If some houses or a village stood where the baron wanted a castle, he simply built on top of them. In Cambridge 25 houses were pulled down to make way for a new castle. In Lincoln the Normans pulled down over 150 houses. A castle was once built in York in only eight days.

Norman barons and their soldiers used motte and bailey castles as a base from which to control the local area. They were built at key points, to guard important roads, ports, river crossings and towns. They became the focus for local trade in the area, which the baron could then tax.

But the problem with castles which go up quickly is that they can be brought down as fast. Wooden fences and buildings can burn, be smashed down – or rot. By as early as 1070, any barons with a bit of time and money began to build their castles in stone.

SOURCE A: *A motte and bailey castle. Each one took 7–14 days to build.*

Keep –
the safest and highest part of the castle. The last line of defence.

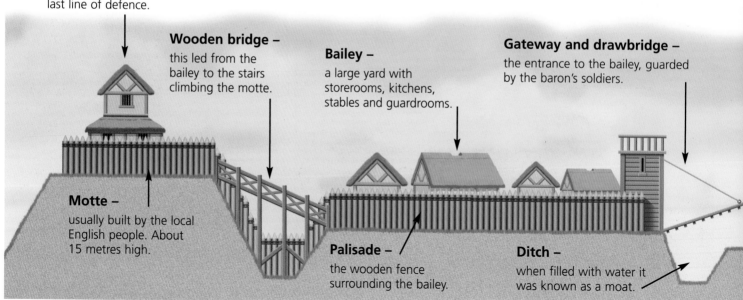

Wooden bridge –
this led from the bailey to the stairs climbing the motte.

Bailey –
a large yard with storerooms, kitchens, stables and guardrooms.

Gateway and drawbridge –
the entrance to the bailey, guarded by the baron's soldiers.

Motte –
usually built by the local English people. About 15 metres high.

Palisade –
the wooden fence surrounding the bailey.

Ditch –
when filled with water it was known as a moat.

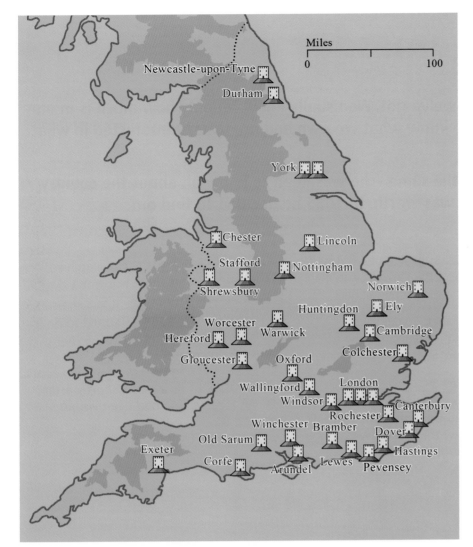

↰ SOURCE B: *Castles built by King William (or on his orders).*

↰ SOURCE C: *The Tower of London, England's first keep built of stone.*

⭐ WISE-UP Words

motte and bailey

Work ～～～．

1 Copy and complete the following paragraph using missing words from the list.

Although William was now _____ of England, he still had the problem of_____ the defeated English. In order to achieve this, one of his favourite tactics was the use of _____. Whenever the English caused him trouble, William would send his _____ to kill all those involved. Another tactic used by William to control the people of England was the building of _____ .

terror

soldiers

castles

King

controlling

2 Why do you think the keep was built on a high earth mound? What advantages would the height give to those in the keep?

3 Imagine you are an angry Englishman who has just led a failed attack on a motte and bailey castle. Describe the obstacles you faced on the way to the keep before you were finally defeated. Remember to include what you think were the weaknesses of the wooden castle.

The Domesday Book

Most of us know how much money we've got. We usually know roughly how much is in our pockets or our savings accounts. We know what we own and are usually interested in what other people own too.

William the Conqueror was exactly the same – he was keen to know all about the country he had conquered and how much it was worth. In 1085 he decided to find out.

The survey

William sent officials all over England to visit each village and ask a series of detailed questions. They interviewed the priest, the steward (the man who organised the farm work in the village) and six elderly villagers.

The officials took a year to visit over 13,000 villages. Soldiers who travelled with them threatened to kill people if they didn't tell the truth. A second group visited the villages later to check they had been telling the truth.

▮▮ PAUSE for Thought
Why do you think that the officials wanted to interview the priest? Why do you think they wanted to talk to the elderly villagers too?

'[The official] made them search so thoroughly that there was not a single yard of land, nor even – it is a shame to tell it but he was not ashamed to do it – one ox, nor a cow, nor a swine that was not set down in his writing.'

↳ SOURCE A: *By a monk shortly after his local village had been visited.*

The book

All the records from the village surveys were sent to Winchester where one man copied it all together in Latin. The surveys filled two huge books and contained approximately two million words.

The book gave William knowledge, and knowledge was a powerful thing. It meant:

- he could work out how much each person in England could afford to pay him in taxes
- he knew exactly how many people he could get to fight for him
- he could settle any quarrels over who owned which bit of land.

However, William never got to see the finished book. While riding his horse in 1087, he slipped forward in his saddle and burst open his bladder. He died in agony. He wouldn't have been able to read it himself anyway – he couldn't read!

> 'At Lincoln there were 970 houses in the time of Edward the Confessor, but 166 were destroyed when the castle was built.'

↰ **SOURCE B:** *An English translation from the Domesday Book.*

> 'Richard holds Birmingham from William. There is land for 6 ploughs; there is one plough in the demesne [lord's land]. There are 5 villeins and 4 bordars and 2 ploughs. There is a wood half a mile long and 4 furlongs broad. In the time of King Edward it was worth 20 shillings and it is still worth the same.'

↰ **SOURCE C:** *Another extract from the Domesday Book. Birmingham is now the second-largest city in England. A furlong is about 200 metres.*

! FACT Winchester or Doomsday?

The book was first called the Winchester Book after the town where it was kept. After about 100 years it started to be called the Domesday Book, after Doomsday – the day of judgement. Like God's judgement on you, people had no right to argue with what the book said.

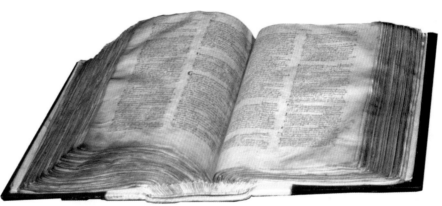

↰ **SOURCE D:** *The Domesday Book still survives today. It is kept in the Public Record Office in London.*

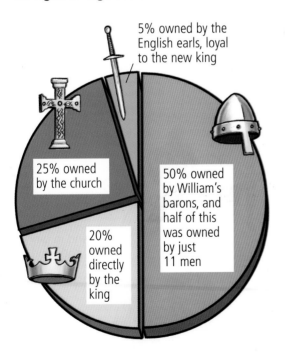

- 5% owned by the English earls, loyal to the new king
- 25% owned by the church
- 50% owned by William's barons, and half of this was owned by just 11 men
- 20% owned directly by the king

↰ **SOURCE E:** *The king owned all the land but he needed help to look after it. This diagram shows who helped the king run his country.*

Work

1 **a** Explain why the Domesday Book was made.

 b Why did it become known as the Domesday Book?

2 Read Source A.

 a What idea does it give us about what the survey was like for villagers?

 b Do you think the monk was happy about King William's survey or not? Explain your answer. Include any clues that might tell us how the monk felt.

3 Read Source B. What does the source tell us about King William's attitude towards the English?

4 According to Sources A and B, what kind of man was William?

5 What does Source E tell us about King William's control of his new country?

The feudal system

Wherever we go, wherever we've been, there's usually someone in control – at home, in the classroom, at work or at a youth club. The person in charge might be a parent, a teacher or a manager. None of us lives in a world where we can do what we want when we want to. Knowing this makes the next two pages very straightforward. By the end you'll understand exactly how King William controlled England.

King William said that all the land in England belonged to him. But England was too large for him to manage by himself, so how did he stay in charge? His answer was to use a system of sharing out the land. The king still owned it, of course, but he could lend large areas of land to people in return for their **loyalty**.

Most of the people he lent the land to had helped him in the Battle of Hastings. He was rewarding them for helping him. 'Feudal' is the Latin word for 'land', so because the new system was based on land, it became known as the **feudal system**.

! FACT **Baron land geography**
King William didn't give his barons their land all in the same place – he carefully dotted it around England. He did this to make it difficult for the barons to build up large armies in the same area. If they became too powerful, he feared they might rebel against him.

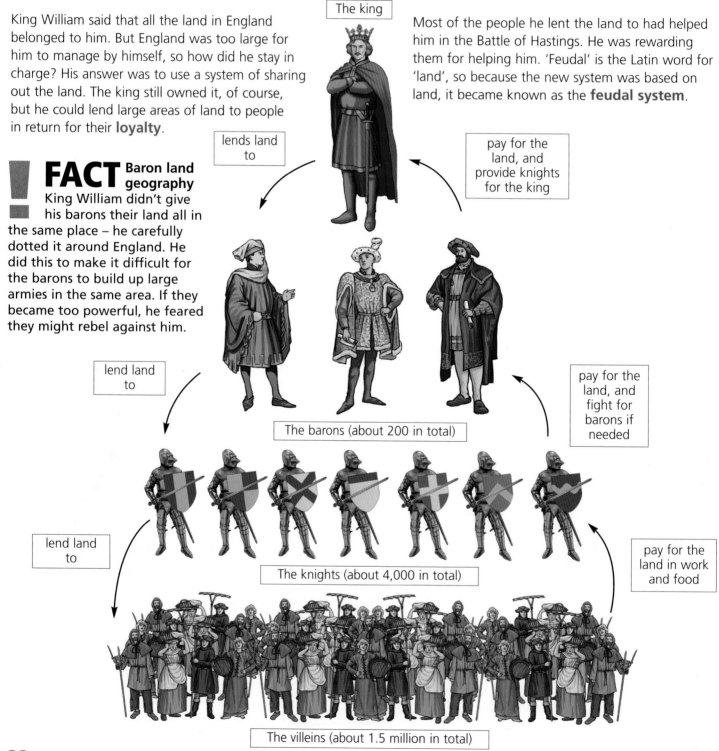

The king

lends land to

pay for the land, and provide knights for the king

lend land to

The barons (about 200 in total)

pay for the land, and fight for barons if needed

lend land to

The knights (about 4,000 in total)

pay for the land in work and food

The villeins (about 1.5 million in total)

A villein's life

A **villein**'s life was very tough. He could never leave the lord's land (the manor) and he had to pay for practically everything. He paid to use the lord's mill, his oven and his brew house. He paid when his son was born and when his daughter got married. Even when he died, the lord was allowed to take his best animal. Some villeins ran away, but their families were fined if they did. If the villein was caught he would be punished too. He might be lucky and avoid capture for a year and a day, and then he would be a **freeman**. The only other way of becoming a freeman was to ask the lord if you could buy your freedom.

Who was the lord?

In the Middle Ages a 'lord' was anyone above you in the feudal system. A villein had several lords, while the barons had just one – the king.

WISE-UP Words

feudal system
freeman
loyalty
villein

Work

1 a How did the feudal system make it easier for King William to control the English?

   b Why was William careful not to give pieces of land to his barons that were too close together?

2 a How could a lord make money from his villeins?

   b Do you think these ways of making money were fair? Explain your answer.

3 William was a clever man. As soon as he became King of England he knew he needed to do the following:
   • reward his followers
   • keep law and order all over England
   • raise money
   • find out the details of how much England was worth.

   a Look at William's four needs. Which one do you think was his priority? Give reasons for your answer.

   b Divide a new page into four boxes. In the middle of each box write one of William's needs. Using words, symbols or diagrams, explain how William solved each of his needs.

↵ SOURCE A: *A knight paying homage to the king. Paying homage meant that he promised to be loyal and to fight for him.*

—— **MISSION ACCOMPLISHED?** ——
• Can you explain why castles were built all over England?
• Can you explain how William collected information about his new kingdom?
• Can you explain what is meant by the term 'feudal system'?

Have you been learning? 1

TASK 1

Look carefully at the following five scenes from the Bayeux Tapestry (Scenes 1, 2, 3, 4 and 5). The pictures are in the right order. Match each picture with the text (Sources A, B, C, D and E), which describes it.

Scene 4

Scene 1

Scene 2

Scene 5

Scene 3

Source A
The Normans surrounded a thousand of those who had chased them and killed them in an instant.

Source B
Yet not daring to fight on equal terms with William, whom they feared more than the King of Norway, they took up position on higher ground on the hill.

Source C
Then it was an arrow which was shot towards the sky, struck Harold above the right eye and that one of his eyes it put out.

Source D
The eager courage of the Normans gave them the first strike – they threw spears and weapons of every kind.

Source E
Three horses were killed under William. Three times he leapt to his feet to avenge the death of his horse.

Now answer these questions.

a What were the three main difference between Harold's and William's warriors at the Battle of Hastings?

b Why do you think the Bayeux Tapestry was made?

c In England in the middle of the eleventh century, why was it so important to use pictures?

34

TASK 2

The passage below doesn't make much sense. It needs capital letters, commas and full stops.

a Copy the passage, adding punctuation as you write.

stone castles were very strong a baron would spend a lot of time and money making sure that his castle was very difficult to break into sometimes the walls were over six metres thick if the people inside the castle had enough food and water they could hold out for weeks maybe even months

attackers used special weapons and tricks to get into a castle and defeat the men inside they might use a trebuchet a battering ram a mangonel or a siege tower at rochester castle in 1216 king john ordered his men to dig under the castle walls fill the tunnel with wood and set fire to it he even ordered 40 fat pigs to be thrown on to the fire the fat burned so well that one of the castle walls began to crack eventually it fell down and king john and his army stormed in

TASK 3

A question mark (?) is used at the end of a sentence which asks a question, for example, 'What time is it please?' It is used instead of a full stop. The next word after a question mark always begins with a capital letter. An exclamation work (!) is used at the end of a sentence or phrase to highlight some sort of special meaning or emphasis. For example, 'I've lost my watch!'

1 Write the following ten sentences or phrases and use either an exclamation mark (!) or a question mark (?) to complete them.

  a How long did it take to build the castle
  b How high are the castle walls
  c We will never get over those wall
  d When was the castle built
  e Why were the castle walls so thick
  f Help, we are being attacked
  g An arrow has hit my leg, I'm in pain
  h What weapons can we use to smash down the walls
  i We shall never surrender
  j Why were castles built all over England

2 Now write down five sentences or phrases about castles or castle life that need an exclamation mark.

TASK 4

Copy a table like the one below. Divide these key words into syllables to help your spelling. Remember that all syllables must include a vowel (a, e, i, o and u), but in some words ('navy' or 'tapestry') the 'y' is classed as a vowel. One word has been done for you.

battle • army • Harold • of • heir • Godwinson • Hastings • arrow • Bayeux • William • housecarl • Tapestry • of • Hardrada • cavalry • Normandy • helmet

One-syllable words	Two-syllable words	Three-syllable words
axe		

TASK 5

If you abbreviate something it means you don't write out all of the words in a phrase or sentence in full, you just shorten some of the words or use the first (initial) letters instead. Abbreviations are a very useful tool if you are asked to make notes on something. For example, 'Her Royal Highness' could be shortened to 'HRH'. Full stops are often used to show where letters are left out, words are shortened or after initials.

1 Write out the following ten words or phrases in full and then try to abbreviate them.
  a William the second
  b Thomas Becket
  c November
  d Forty metres
  e His Majesty
  f Lancashire
  g Thirteenth century
  h Volume two
  i Roman Catholic
  j Member of Parliament

2 Now try to work out what the following abbreviations mean:
  a UK
  b 4th
  c @
  d BC
  e Henry II
  f C11th
  g St. Mark ch2 v 4
  h E.g.
  i Dec
  j West Mids

3 Can you think of ten more abbreviations that are used today?

How did castles develop?

MISSION OBJECTIVES

- To understand how and why castles changed after 1066.

The earliest castles were built of wood – and were built very quickly. They were built to keep out enemies and to keep people, horses and treasures safe. They dominated river crossings, roadways and towns and were used as a base from which the baron could control the local population (see Source A).

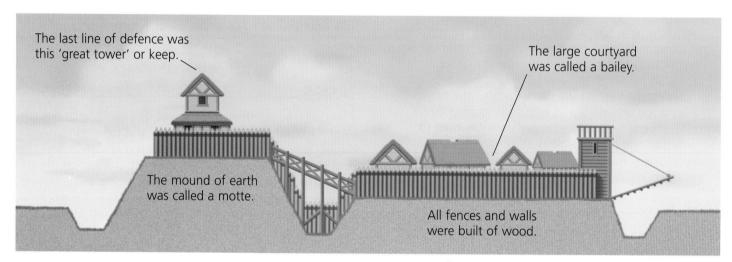

The last line of defence was this 'great tower' or keep.

The large courtyard was called a bailey.

The mound of earth was called a motte.

All fences and walls were built of wood.

The early wooden castles were good at reminding the English people that they had been beaten, but they were very weak against a determined attack. The wooden walls could quite easily be chopped or burnt down, or just climbed over with ladders. So as early as 1070, a few lords with the time, money and suitable location began to build their castles in stone (see Source B).

SOURCE A: *A picture of a very early motte and bailey castle. On the orders of King William, hundreds of these were built all over England in the years after 1066.*

SOURCE B: *An early stone castle. The massive square keep towered over the countryside, striking fear or respect into the hearts of those who saw it.*

The wooden tower was knocked down and a stone keep built instead. It was much larger than the wooden one and contained most of the castle's important rooms – the lord's personal apartment, the kitchen, chapel, main hall, stores, guardroom and dungeon.

A wide, deep ditch called a moat. This made it very difficult for attackers to get close to the castle walls, and if they tried to tunnel under the walls, the tunnel would fill with water.

A well-guarded bridge.

The wooden fence was pulled down and a tall stone one built in its place. This was called a curtain wall.

The curtain wall was often wide enough for soldiers to walk along the top.

Battlements for soldiers to hide behind when they fired arrows.

If a castle's outer walls were really strong though, sometimes the lord didn't even bother with the keep at all. They were dark, noisy, smoky places anyway, and lacked privacy, so sometimes a lord would build all the rooms, buildings and accommodation he needed within the bailey itself. He would then strengthen the curtain wall with extra towers and build an especially tough entrance called a **barbican** (see Sources C and D).

WISE-UP Words

barbican

↵ **SOURCE C:** *In this castle there is no great tower or keep. Instead, the main rooms are built up against the thick strong outer walls.*

Defending soldiers

Hot water

Two wall towers, containing guard rooms for the soldiers

These were known as murder holes

Portcullis made from iron

Attackers

↵ **SOURCE D:** *A gatehouse or barbican.*

37

For a while then, in the early 1200s, things seemed impossible for the attacker. The walls were so thick (sometimes five metres thick) and so well defended that breaking through them would have taken forever. And if, by some miracle, an attacking army got through the wall and saw a keep in front of them, it was usually too high to climb up and the defenders would be up there firing arrows, throwing rocks and boiling water down onto them.

The main door of the keep was on the first floor level too, with only a steep wooden stairway up to it so that attackers couldn't batter down the door anyway.

At first, the only way to capture the keep was to 'lay siege'. This meant sitting outside and waiting until the defenders ran out of food, water and weapons.

Castle evolution

However, it didn't take long before attackers came up with new ideas that would change the shape of castles. It was discovered that the square corners of the towers – and the keep – were weak and could be undermined. This meant they collapsed if attackers dug tunnels underneath them. Also, better and better machines were being designed that could throw huge boulders at the walls and batter them. So the defenders had to think up new ideas to protect themselves and came up with the **concentric castle**.

The concentric castle was an idea brought back by the knights fighting abroad in the Holy Lands around Jerusalem. They were more regular in shape than earlier castles and used water defences wherever possible. The towers were all round because they were harder to undermine by soldiers digging underneath them, and each set of walls decreased in height so that archers on the upper walls could shoot over the heads of the soldiers below (see Sources E and F).

SOURCE E:
Concentric castle. ↴

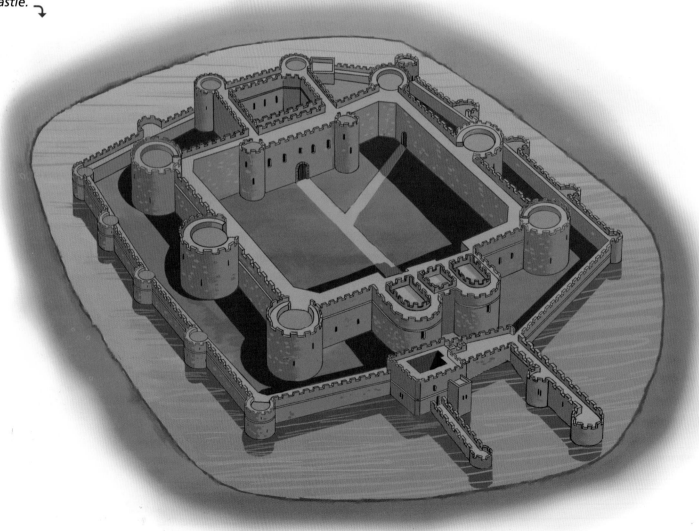

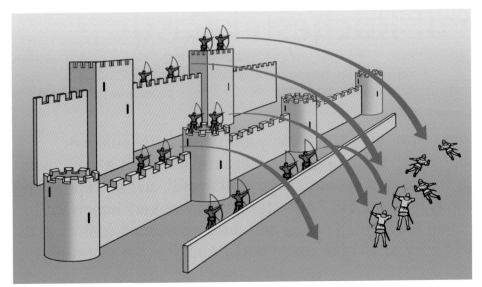

↵ **SOURCE F:** *How walls of different heights helped the defenders.*

The great age of castle building began to decline in the early 1400s. The country began to become more peaceful and there was no need for such strong expensive castles to be built. Instead, they were changed and modified to become lavish homes, and new ones were built for comfort first and defence second (see Source H).

↰ **SOURCE G:** *Caerphilly Castle, Wales.*

↵ **SOURCE H:** *A picture of Herstmonceux Castle in East Sussex. After 1400, most castles were no longer heavily fortified. This one had brick walls and large windows.*

___MISSION ACCOMPLISHED?___

• Can you explain five differences between an early motte and bailey castle and a concentric castle?

The siege of Rochester Castle

- To remember at least five weapons, methods or tactics used to get into a castle under siege.

In 1216, a group of rebel barons and more than 100 heavily armed soldiers took over Rochester Castle. They weren't happy with their king, John, because he wasn't a very good soldier. He lost so many battles in France that he was called 'softsword', and he kept asking the barons for more and more money in taxes. But Rochester Castle was very important for King John. It guarded one of the main roads into London and the king needed control of it! So what did the king do? How did he try to win the castle back? And how did 40 fat pigs come to his rescue?

Greek fire –
a mixture of tar, oil and sulphur which could not be put out with water. Only urine could put the fire out!

Battering ram –
a tree trunk hanging on a wooden frame, protected by an animal skin roof.

Siege tower –
a large wooden tower protected by animal skins. In 1216 over 200 soldiers hid in one large tower when attacking Kenilworth Castle.

Mangonel –
another machine used to fire rocks at the castle.

Sappers –
specialist soldiers who could fill in a moat with logs, stones or soil. Also they could dig under a wall or tower and collapse it.
The wooden cover they hid under was called a tortoise.

Archers –
a skilled archer could fire an arrow over 200 metres, or even straight through the arrow slits in the castle walls.

Trebuchet –
could fire rocks or quicklime. Sometimes rotting animal corpses were even fired into the castle.

Rochester Castle was very well defended. The outer walls were over three metres thick and the walls of the main tower were over 34 metres high. At first the king decided to lay siege to the castle. From the French word 'siège', meaning 'a seat', a siege is when attackers literally sit down and wait. They stop anyone getting in or out of the castle – and when the food runs out, the people inside have to give up and surrender, or starve to death.

However, after a few weeks the king realised that he was wasting his time. The barons had enough food and water to hold out for weeks, maybe months. So the king scrapped the siege and instructed his army to use some of the latest weapons – battering rams, mangonels and trebuchets – to get in and defeat the naughty barons.

But as hard as they tried, King John's soldiers just couldn't smash down the castle's thick walls. After a few weeks, things were getting desperate for the king; he received news that another group of rebels were about to come and help the ones trapped inside the castle, so he needed another plan and quickly!

The king's clever idea was to instruct his sappers to dig a tunnel, held up with wooden props under the castle walls. He then sent out his soldiers to find 40 fat pigs and bring them to his camp. He told his sappers to set fire to the wooden props supporting the tunnel and throw the pigs onto the fire. The fat burned so well that the tunnel caved in and the wall above began to crack. Eventually it fell down and the king's army stormed in! The siege of Rochester Castle was over – thanks to 40 fat pigs!

Rochester Castle.

▌**FACT** Don't be a traitor!

King John didn't punish the rebel barons as severely as many thought he would. He needed their money, after all, and decided it would be best if they were kept alive so that he could tax them heavily. However, he did get his revenge on one man who changed sides halfway through the siege and joined the rebels. What did King John do to the unfortunate young man? He ordered his hands and feet to be cut off.

Work ⌒.

1 Why did the barons inside Rochester Castle rebel against King John?

2 a What is meant by the term 'lay seige'?

  b In your own words, explain how King John finally managed to get into Rochester Castle?

3 Now you have read about the seige of Rochester Castle, it's time to put your knowledge about attacking and defending castles into practice.

The year is 1304 and Stirling Castle is under siege! In pairs, you are to imagine the events that took place in the final week of the siege.

  a One person is to take the role of the attacker. Think about what tricks and weapons you could use to get in. The other person is to take the role of the baron, defending his castle. Think about what defences you have for keeping them out.

  b In pairs, discuss the possible events during this last week.

  c Write a siege diary from the point of view of your character. Include all the events of that week. How the siege ends is up to you.

─ **MISSION ACCOMPLISHED?** ─

- Do you know the difference between a seige tower and a trebuchet?
- Can you explain how King John got into Rochester Castle?

Who lived in a castle like this?

_____ MISSION OBJECTIVES _____
• To understand what day-to-day life in a castle was like and know the names and jobs of the people who lived there.

A castle was very busy because it was a lord or baron's home – so the castle was full of people who looked after him, such as servants, cooks and entertainers. But it was also a local centre of government used as a base from which the lord or baron ruled the local area. On behalf of the king, a lord or baron would be expected to collect taxes, arrest criminals, prevent rebellion and guard against invasion. So lots of different people were needed to do this. A castle was rather like a town hall and a police station all rolled into one, and was always full of people busily going about their business. Who were the castle's most important and interesting inhabitants?

I am the baron. I own the castle and all the land around it. I even own the peasants working on my land. I have other castles in different parts of the country too. I spend my money on fantastic food, beautiful wall hangings, gold and silver jewellery and entertaining my friends.

I am the baron's wife, one of the few women who live in the castle. I look after our children, with help from my personal servants known as ladies in waiting. I can sew, sing and play musical instruments, so I can impress my husband's important friends when they come and visit.

As the steward, I am responsible for all the servants – the cooks, butlers, serving staff, gardeners, even the gong farmer!

I stink. I'm the gong farmer that's why! My job is to clean out all the garderobes or toilets.

I am the constable and my main focus is security. The safety of the castle is my responsibility so I make sure the soldiers control who or what comes in and out of this place. I actually run the whole castle when the lord is away.

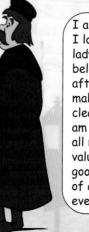

I am the marshall. I look after the horses and carts, the blacksmiths, stonemasons and carpenters.

I am the chamberlain. I look after my lord and lady's rooms and all their belongings. I also look after their clothes and make sure the servants clean them properly. I am trusted to look after all my lord's money and valuables. I make sure good accounts are kept of all the taxes paid and every penny spent.

I am an **oubliette** (forgotten prisoner) and have stolen from the baron. My body is on display as a warning to others. My body will stay here for months. Birds and maggots will eat my flesh until only bones are left.

There is so much work to be done around here and we are too busy to stop and explain exactly what we do. As **servants**, we are the ones who cook, clean, wash, serve, tidy, fetch and carry. Few of us even have proper rooms, so we just sleep anywhere we can.

I'm the castle **jester**. Sometimes people call me the fool. My job is to tell funny stories and sing rude songs. Even my clothes are silly.

My job as a **sheriff** is to arrest criminals, collect taxes and make sure people keep the laws. I don't live in the castle, but visit it often to meet with the lord.

Work

```
        6
1       ▼
  1▶ □□□□□□□□
  2▶ □□□□□□
3▶ □□□□□□□
  4▶ □□□□□□□□
  5▶ □□□□□
```

Clues

1 Forgotten prisoner
2 Baron's wife
3 Looks after the horses and carts
4 Defenders of the castle
5 Works 40 days a year
6 Now read down the grid and write a sentence or two about this person.

2 Choose one of the characters from the castle. Imagine that they have fallen from the battlements by accident! It's your job to recruit someone to fill their post. Write a job advert to find a replacement. Remember to include a full job description and the skills required for this post.

I've got 21 days to go! As a **knight**, my main job is to protect my lord. I do this for 40 days a year because the lord gave me some land. I use men who live on my land as soldiers to help me. When my 40 days are over another knight who lives nearby will come and do his duty.

We work for him! Our job as **soldiers** is to defend the castle and protect the lord when he travels around.

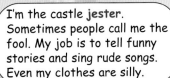

MISSION ACCOMPLISHED?

• Can you describe five different jobs in a typical castle?

Castles around the world

- To understand where and why castles were built in other places in the world, aside from England.

Castles and fortresses were built all over the world during the Middle Ages. Most were built near rivers for the water supply, or to guard borders and coastlines. In some countries (like France, Spain and England) you can find clusters of castles all within a few miles of each other, which often indicates that the area was a trouble spot in the Middle Ages.

Castles were built in many different styles. In France, for example, castles usually had tall pointed roofs to their towers. In Spain, the castles had decorated brickwork which reflected the influence of the Muslims (called Moors) who ruled the area for many years. Outside Europe, the main castle building area was Japan. Here, castles had stone bases with wooden keeps with overhanging roofs. The map shows just a few of the key castles around the world.

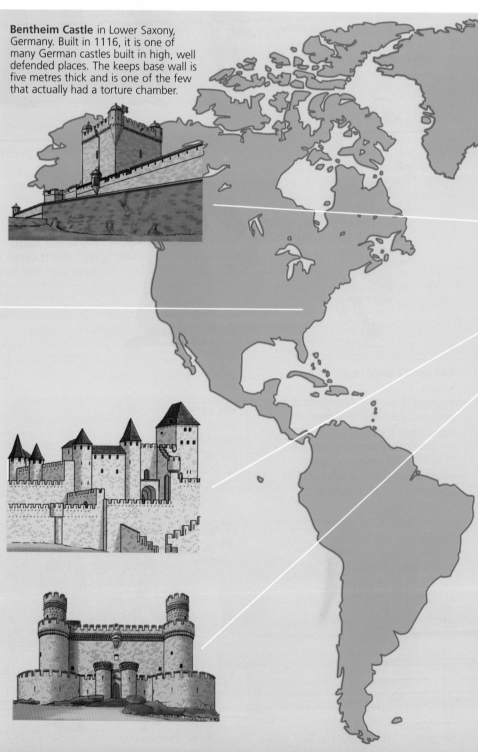

Bentheim Castle in Lower Saxony, Germany. Built in 1116, it is one of many German castles built in high, well defended places. The keeps base wall is five metres thick and is one of the few that actually had a torture chamber.

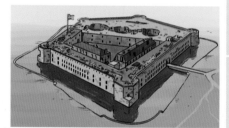

Fort Delaware in the USA was built as a fortress in 1859 during the American Civil War. It is the closest America has to a real castle!

Carcassonne Castle in France. Built in the twelfth and thirteenth centuries, this style of castle, with roofs capping each tower, is typical of castles all over mainland Europe. It is a style copied by Walt Disney!

El Real de Manzanares in Spain. Built in 1475 in a style known as moorish, after the Muslim Arabs called moors who ruled Spain for many years.

Work

1 a

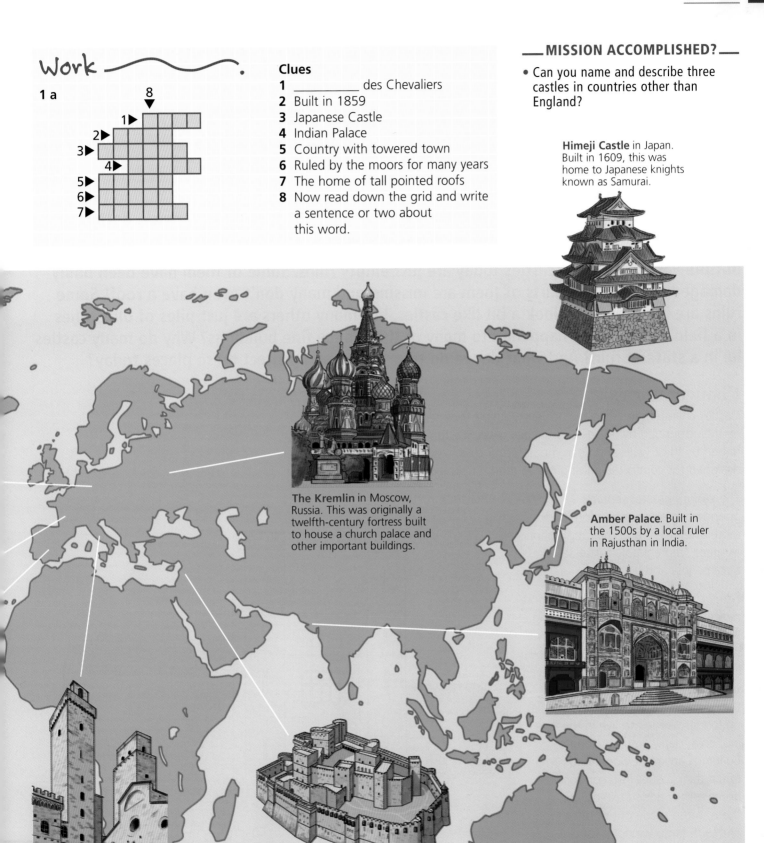

Clues

1 _____ des Chevaliers
2 Built in 1859
3 Japanese Castle
4 Indian Palace
5 Country with towered town
6 Ruled by the moors for many years
7 The home of tall pointed roofs
8 Now read down the grid and write a sentence or two about this word.

MISSION ACCOMPLISHED?

• Can you name and describe three castles in countries other than England?

Himeji Castle in Japan. Built in 1609, this was home to Japanese knights known as Samurai.

The Kremlin in Moscow, Russia. This was originally a twelfth-century fortress built to house a church palace and other important buildings.

Amber Palace. Built in the 1500s by a local ruler in Rajusthan in India.

In Northern Italy, rich families often lived in towns rather than castles but dotted tall stone towers around the local area to defend themselves if ever they came under attack. **San Gimignano** in Tuscany still has 13 medieval towers – originally there were 76!

Krak des Chevaliers in Syria is one of the most famous medieval castles in the world and the best example of a crusader castle. It was built by warrior monks at a time when Crusaders and Saracens (a general name for Turks and Arabs) were building massive fortresses all over the Holy Land.

Where have all our castles gone?

The great age of castle building was between 1066 and about 1350. It was during this time that many of Britain's most famous castles were completed, including Warwick, Rochester, Kenilworth, Conway and, of course, the Tower of London.

But the vast majority of castles today are just empty ruins. Some of them have been badly damaged so that large parts of them are missing and many don't even have a roof! Some ruins are huge, and still look a bit like castles, but many others are just piles of old stones in a field. So what has happened to many of these once fine buildings? Why do many castles lie in a state of ruin? And what do we do to preserve and protect these places today?

Changes to castles

Castles changed greatly over the years. Simple wooden towers on a mound of earth surrounded by fences and ditches gave way to massive stone castles ringed by thick walls and deep moats. Later castles were more like palaces, designed for comfortable living rather than for protection and controlling land.

The castle's greatest enemy – gunpowder – was used more and more after 1350 and their reputation as great, impregnable fortresses became less and less.

After 1500, our country became more peaceful and there was less fighting. Rich castle-owning nobles lost power to the king, and stopped fighting over local plots of land so they didn't need the same level of protection from their homes. To put it simply, people no longer needed to live in these big, cold, dark, draughty, damp buildings anymore. Some lords made their castles into comfortable homes. They added extensions to them, often made out of brick and with large windows, and made pretty gardens around their castles (see Source A). Other lords and barons moved out of their castles and built smaller, more comfortable homes nearby. They let the castles fall to ruin (see Source B).

SOURCE A

SOURCE B

✚ Hungry for **MORE**

There is probably a medieval castle or some ruins in a town near you. Research and make a presentation on the castle, including:
- Who built it and when?
- Did any sieges take place there?
- Find out if it has any special features used to protect it from attack.
- Try to find out a little bit about who lived in the castle.
- Have you visited it? What was it like? How did you find out about its past?

Castles today

There are literally hundreds of castles dotted all over Britain. Whilst lots are now ruins, some have undergone dramatic restoration and have been converted into hotels and conference centres. Others are still privately owned and are used as homes.

Many, though, are looked after by groups and organisations such as English Heritage, Cadw and the National Trust. You can go and visit some of our finest castles, wander around the grounds, look through the display areas and gaze at medieval artefacts, models and old suits of armour. Sometimes there are demonstrations by knights on horseback or archers shooting arrows. Often they have a snack bar and a shop where you can buy a souvenir of your visit. Every year thousands of peopld visit Britain's castles – clearly there is still a huge interest in the way people lived in castles.

Work

1 In your own words explain why after 1350 castles were used less and less, and why many turned to ruins.

2 Think for yourself. How do organisations like English Heritage, Cadw and the National Trust look after Britain's castles today? You might like to discuss answers to this in a group before you write them down.

3 Look at Source A. Imagine you are an estate agent with the job of selling the castle. Create a set of notes to go with the picture to help sell the property. You need to make sure you include why castles were built in Britain to begin with, what role they played in medieval history and how the castle has been changed, developed and extended over the years. You might want to add more pictures to your sales information.

_____ **MISSION ACCOMPLISHED?** _____

- Can you tell someone why people stopped building and living in castles and what you might expect to see if you visited a castle today?

↵ **SOURCE C:** *Raglan Castle.*

HOW RELIGIOUS WERE PEOPLE IN THE MIDDLE AGES?

Today, there are many different religions in England. Many people consider themselves Christians but only around three people in every hundred go to church on a Sunday. Things were very different in medieval England and religion was much more important in people's lives. Over the next few pages, you will learn about the role of the Church, how and why people worked for God and why people became pilgrims.

1: Religion and the Church

MISSION OBJECTIVES

- To understand how and why religion affected everyday life in medieval England.
- To understand how powerful the Church was and how it used its power.

In England during the Middle Ages, nearly everyone believed in God. They followed the Roman Catholic religion led by the **Pope** in Rome. It was the only religion in England at this time. People also believed that heaven and hell were very real places – as real as France or Spain to us. And whether you ended up in heaven or hell depended on how you lived your life whilst on Earth. So what did this mean for the ordinary medieval villager? What could they do to get into heaven and avoid hell? And how else did the Church feature in their lives?

Hell to pay

People used religion to explain things. If they fell and broke their arm or caught a nasty infection, it was a punishment from God. If a baby died, it was because God wanted it. For most ordinary people, life was terribly hard and heaven seemed a warm, comforting reward for all their suffering on Earth.

If people were bad, however, there would be no reward in the **afterlife** – quite the opposite in fact! As well as being told about hell by the priest, there were pictures, statues and stained glass windows to remind people what hell was like. Huge **doom paintings** showed angels welcoming people into heaven and devils pulling wicked people into hell and torturing them in all sorts of horrific ways.

Church services were held in Latin, which ordinary people couldn't understand! There was a very good chance that the priest wouldn't understand what he was saying either – he would just learn the services by heart! You couldn't read the Bible unless you could read Latin – the Pope banned it from being translated into English.

How was the Church organised?

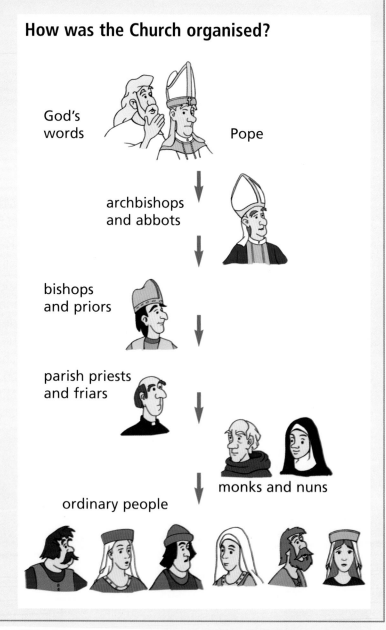

God's words → Pope

archbishops and abbots

bishops and priors

parish priests and friars

monks and nuns

ordinary people

The heart of the village

The biggest building in a town or village would be the church. Unlike today, churches were very noisy, sometimes hectic places. As most people's homes were tiny, smelly huts full of smoke and animals, they didn't want to spend much time there! The church served as a meeting place for people, somewhere they could all sit comfortably and catch up on local gossip.

The price of religion

The church didn't come for free. The villagers had to give one tenth of all the food they grew to the parish priest. This was known as the **tithe**. As you can imagine, the villagers were often unhappy about this, especially when the harvest was bad. You also had to pay the church when you died! The priest was entitled to receive the second best animal of anyone that died in the village. Worshipping God and trying to get into heaven was an expensive business.

↰ SOURCE A: *This section of a doom painting dates from the 16th century, and is on a church wall in Voronet, Romania.*

'They say the priest was away for six weeks and made no arrangements for a substitute. He spends his time in taverns, and his tongue is loosened to the great scandal of everyone. He is living with a woman, Margaret, and he cannot read or write so cannot look after his parishioners' souls.'

↰ SOURCE B: *By the Bishop of Hereford in 1347. He took evidence from people as he visited the local villages.*

WISE-UP Words

afterlife
doom paintings
Pope   tithe

Work

1 a Copy and complete the following paragraph.

Everyone believed in _____ and

went to _____ in the Middle Ages.

The local church was the _____

building, and would have been very

_____ and _____.

People tried to lead good lives because they wanted

to go to _____. They were afraid

of _____.

1 b Villagers had to give the church one tenth of their harvest as a tithe. What is this as a percentage?

2 Study Source A.

a Why was it important to have pictures and paintings on church walls in the Middle Ages? Clue: Think about the language used by the priest in his services.

b What was the purpose of a doom painting? How do you think these kinds of paintings might affect the way someone behaved after leaving church?

c Draw your own doom painting. Remember, it's got to tell people what will happen to them in heaven and hell, and must not include any words.

3 Describe who was in overall control of religion in Medieval England and how his message was passed on to ordinary people.

_____ **MISSION ACCOMPLISHED?** _____

• Can you tell someone what religion everyone followed in medieval England?

• Do you know what people thought would happen to them if they didn't do what the Church said?

• Can you give a reason why people used the church that had nothing to do with God or religion?

Some men decided to devote their whole lives to God. They left their families, homes and possessions and moved into a monastery as a monk. But what did they do when they got there? What rules did they live by to please God? How did they help the rest of society? And what made so many men become monks?

2: A day in the life of a monk

MISSION OBJECTIVES

- To understand how and why religion affected everyday life in medieval England.
- To understand how powerful the Church was and how it used its power.

Why take up the habit?

Monks first arrived in England in the sixth century, when Saint Benedict built the first monastery. In 1066, there were around 1000 monks in England – but this number quickly increased after William's invasion. By 1300, there were over 12 000 monks in England – meaning that out of every 150 people, one was a monk!

A monk's life was not an easy one. It was dominated by prayer – every three hours – day and night! They had to live by a strict set of rules set down by Saint Benedict.

A good monk must:

Spend his life in service to God.

Give away all of his property.

Obey the abbot (head of the monastery) at all times.

Wear a habit (robe), sandals and shave the top of his head.

Stay in the monastery until he dies.

Signed

Saint Benedict

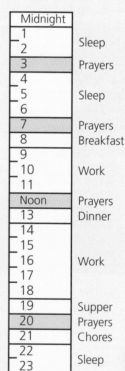

Midnight	
1	Sleep
2	
3	Prayers
4	
5	Sleep
6	
7	Prayers
8	Breakfast
9	
10	Work
11	
Noon	Prayers
13	Dinner
14	
15	
16	Work
17	
18	
19	Supper
20	Prayers
21	Chores
22	
23	Sleep
Midnight	

↳ **SOURCE A:** *To us, the life of a medieval monk seems pretty tough. But to many monks, joining the monastery was an escape from everyday pressures. Read Source B.*

✚ Hungry for MORE

Not all monks followed the rules laid down by Saint Benedict. As well as Benedictines, there were Cistercians, Cluniacs, Augustinians, Premonstrations and Carthusians. Franciscan friars arrived in England in the thirteenth century. They were monks who did not live in monasteries but spent their time travelling around. See if you can find out more about the rules that these different orders lived by.

↰ **SOURCE B:** *By a monk from Rievaulx Abbey in 1170.*

! FACT What's that in the back of the picture?

Most art was religious. The illuminated manuscripts, painted by the monks, mostly showed Bible stories – although sometimes they doodled scenes from everyday life. Rich families sometimes paid artists to paint pictures especially for them but these usually showed religious scenes too. It was not unknown for an artist to be paid to paint the birth of Jesus – and put the rich nobleman's family in the background.

★ WISE-UP Words

chronicles
illuminated   manuscripts
monastery   monk
scriptorium

↰ **SOURCE C:** *Large monasteries like this housed dozens of monks and were called abbeys.*

Illuminating work

Monks were probably the best educated people in medieval society and monasteries were important centres of learning. They acted as libraries for ancient books and **manuscripts**. Monks not only read these books but made sure the knowledge wasn't lost by copying them. This took place in a special room called a **scriptorium**, a long narrow hall with booths placed against windows to help the monks see what they were doing. Valuable books were chained to the desk to prevent them being damaged if they were knocked off. Sometimes monks wrote their own books called **chronicles**. They also often **illuminated** their books with tiny, beautiful paintings around the edges of the page and on the capital letters.

↰ **SOURCE D:** *This example of an illuminated manuscript comes from the Lindisfarne Gospels.*

Work

1 Give as many reasons as you can to explain why some men became monks.

2 Look at the typical monk's day, and then answer the following questions.

   a At what time:
   • did monks get up for prayers?
   • did they go to bed?

   b Look at Source B. Explain why some men were tempted to become monks.

3 Using Source D as a guide, make your own illuminated manuscript. On the manuscript, explain why monks copied books out by hand and why this was important.

MISSION ACCOMPLISHED?

• Can you tell somebody why some men decided to become monks?
• Do you know how a monk spent an average day?
• Could you explain how monasteries preserved and spread knowledge?

It wasn't just men who wanted to devote their lives to God, women did too. They became nuns and lived in nunneries, mostly followed the rules of Saint Benedict, and lived lives fairly similar to monks. There were not as many nuns as monks though and they hardly ever worked with books or manuscripts. So what did they do instead? How and why did women become nuns? And how did they help the rest of society?

3: Was it fun to be a nun?

MISSION OBJECTIVES

- To understand why some women became nuns and what their lives involved.
- To understand how they helped the rest of society.

My name is Sister Emily and I'm 16 years old. When I was born, my mother and I nearly died. My father prayed to God and promised Him that I would spend my life doing His work if I lived. I did, so when I was a very young girl, my father kept his promise and handed me over to the Sisters with a **dowry**.

My name is Sister Ursula and I'm 22 years old. When it became time for me to marry, I told my father that I didn't want a husband – I wanted to become a nun. That way, my education would continue and I would have responsibilities and jobs that are far more interesting than being a wife and mother. My father gave a dowry to the nunnery and I donated my silver necklace that belonged to my grandfather.

My name is Sister Winifred and I am 55 years old. I became a nun when my husband died two years ago. I decided to dedicate the rest of my life to God and gave all of my money and belongings, including my house, to the nunnery. Now I have nothing to worry about other than pleasing God and doing His work.

! FACT

Not every young woman was thrilled at the prospect of a life devoted to God. In 1318, a nun called Joanna from Clementhorpe Nunnery, faked her own death and staged her own funeral in an attempt to escape becoming consecrated!

Women became nuns for a number of different reasons and at various different ages. Look at the stories of the three nuns above.

The Brides of Christ

After living by the rules of Saint Benedict for five years, nuns were **consecrated**. This involved a ceremony that was very similar to a wedding. The nun would have a ring placed on her finger and she wore a wedding crown as she took her vows. From then on, she would be seen as being married to God.

The daily life of a nun was very similar to that of a monk – based around prayer and chores. But rather than working in the scriptorium, nuns saw it as their duty to look after the sick (see Source B). The Church built 160 new hospitals between 1205 and 1300, many of which were attached to nunneries.

SOURCE A: *A picture of nuns looking after the sick in their nunnery. Nuns or sisters often attended to the sick – that's why senior nurses in hospitals today are known as 'sisters'.*

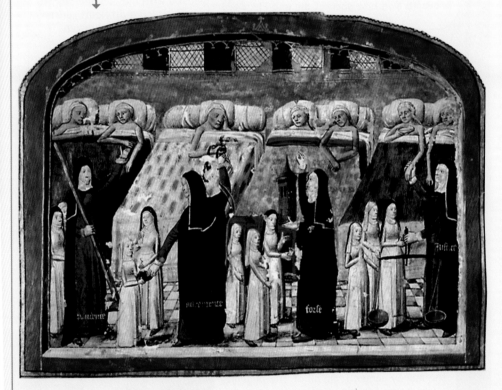

The word hospital comes from the Latin word hospitalis, which means 'a place for guests'. Originally, they were just intended as places where visitors could sleep for the night but people soon began to take their sick relatives to the nunneries. It was the nun's duty to care for the unwell and the hospitals soon grew in number and size.

WISE-UP Words

consecrated
dowry

" Care for the sick stands before everything. You must help them as Christ would, whom you really help by helping them. Also, you must be patient with them and you will gain quarter merit with God. The sick should not be neglected at any single point. "

SOURCE B: *The rules for Benedictine monks, AD534.*

Work

1 Give at least two different reasons why some women became nuns.

2 Explain why nuns were sometimes called the 'Brides of Christ'.

3 Imagine you are a young nun. Write a letter to your parents that explains how you are serving God and helping people. Your teacher will show you how to set it out.

MISSION ACCOMPLISHED?

- Can you give somebody at least two reasons why women became nuns in medieval England?
- Could you explain why you would be glad that there were nuns, if you were alive in the Middle Ages?

4: How did pilgrims progress?

Monasteries and nunneries were not just centres of learning and hospitals, they also had another very important use. Going on a pilgrimage – a long journey to visit an important religious site – was very popular in medieval England.

Monasteries and nunneries acted as hotels for weary travellers, making sure they received food and shelter. But what kind of people went on pilgrimages? What were their motives? Where did they go and how did the Church help them on their way?

MISSION OBJECTIVES

- To understand what a pilgrimage was.
- To know the different reasons why people became pilgrims.
- To know how pilgrims travelled and survived on the road.

Hello there **pilgrim**, my name is Andrew. I am ashamed to say that I have been ordered to come on this pilgrimage by my parish priest. I stole one of my neighbour's animals and to prove how sorry I am and to pray for forgiveness, I have come here to save from myself from hell! Hopefully, the hardship and cost of my journey will prove to God how sorry I am and He will forgive me.

God bless you pilgrim. My name is James and I am a fellow traveller. I decided to set out on this journey to see a bit of the world – I had never left my village before! I also wanted to spend more time thinking about God and praying – ordinary life just seems to get in the way. I have chosen to come to Glastonbury because it is a very long way from my home near York. Hopefully, God will be pleased with me for deciding to come on such a difficult journey and I will go to heaven.

My name is Brother Matthew and I am a monk here at Glastonbury Abbey. According to the Domesday Book, we are the richest abbey in the country. Most of the money comes from all of the pilgrims who come to visit us. We are blessed because it is on this very spot that Saint Thomas Aquinas first brought Christianity to England. Please feel free to chat to our pilgrims and hear their stories.

‖ PAUSE for Thought

Although some women did go on pilgrimages, it was quite unusual. Why do you think this was?

The fastest way to get around was by horse, and not all pilgrims could afford that! Because travelling was so slow, the average pilgrimage lasted about a year. Whilst on the trip, a pilgrim was seen as working for God and they were free from the usual rules of society. They didn't have to pay tax, repay any debts, couldn't be arrested and couldn't have their belongings confiscated. In fact, people were told to entertain, feed and help pilgrims as it would please God.

SOURCE A: *A modern artist's idea of how a medieval pilgrim might have looked.*

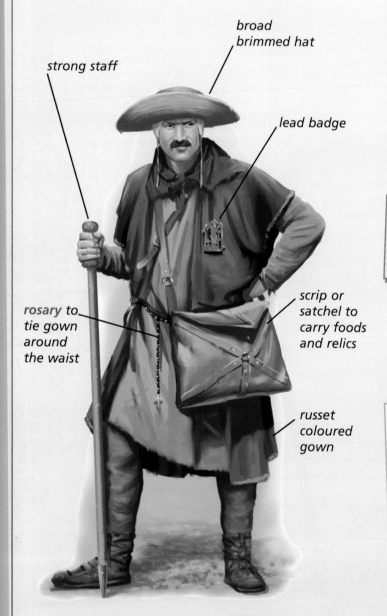

broad brimmed hat

strong staff

lead badge

rosary to tie gown around the waist

scrip or satchel to carry foods and relics

russet coloured gown

Although pilgrims were supposed to be protected by the Church, Britain's roads were lonely and dangerous places. Because of this, pilgrims tended to travel in groups with armed soldiers as bodyguards. Guide books, telling pilgrims the best places to stop and eat, were on sale and some people organised groups for a fee – just like travel agents today.

Pilgrimages became so popular that the towns, monasteries, nunneries and markets along the most popular routes began to make a lot of money. In order to prove that they had visited an important site or **shrine**, pilgrims bought lead or pewter badges to wear on their hats or coats.

They also bought little lead flasks filled with holy water back from their travels. This water would then be sprinkled on their fields to guarantee a good harvest or on a sick relative to make them better. Some pilgrimage sites sold **relics** to the visitors. This could be part of a bone from the body of a saint who had died there or a piece of his coffin. People hoped that some of the holiness of the saint would rub off on them if they carried a relic.

'And specially from every shires ende
Of Engelond to Caunterbury they wende,
The hooly blissful martir for to seke,
That hem hath holpen whan that they were seeke.'

SOURCE B: *An extract from 'The Canterbury Tales', a very long poem about pilgrims written by Geoffrey Chaucer in the 14th century.*

'In the summer of 1143, William of Lythwood returns to Shrewsbury in a coffin... his pilgrimage at last at an end. William's young attendant, Elave, accompanies the body and sets about trying to secure a burial place on the grounds of the Abbey of St. Peter and St. Paul.'

SOURCE C: *From 'The Heretic's Apprentice' by Ellis Peters, a modern novel about a medieval detective monk.*

Pilgrims visited places where they thought miracles had happened. The people who had witnessed or performed these miracles were often made **saints** by the Pope and there would be a town or building named after them. Often, the saints were buried near the site of where the miracle was supposed to have taken place, and pilgrims would pray to the saints and hope that some miracle would take place in their lives too. Other places that pilgrims visited had relics that they believed belonged to Jesus or his family.

Although there were hundreds of places for pilgrims to choose, some sites were more popular than others. Glastonbury was very popular because people believed it was the place where Christianity was introduced to England. Saint Joseph of Arimathea was believed to have come to England and at that spot was supposed to have struck the ground with his staff. Legend says that a thorn bush, known as the Holy Thorn, grew instantly out of the ground that he touched! Others headed for Walsingham in Norfolk because they believed that there was a jar of the Virgin Mary's breast milk there!

⌐ SOURCE D: *A pilgrim's lead badge*

The town of St Albans was named after a man who helped a priest escape from the Romans. Alban was killed for his actions but a spring is said to have miraculously appeared on the spot where his head was chopped off. The eyes of his executioner are also said to have dropped out!

Work

1 Match the motive to the pilgrim.

Pilgrim	Motive for pilgrimage
Jonathan	To cure him of his illness.
James	As a punishment for committing a crime
Andrew	To have a religious holiday.
Daniel	To guarantee a good harvest.

2 Why do you think that many pilgrims preferred to visit shrines that were very difficult to get to?

3 Give two reasons why pilgrims bought lead and pewter badges from sites they had visited.

4 What else did pilgrims take home from pilgrimages? How did they think that this would help them?

5 a Try to read Source B. Can you work out where Chaucer says that the Pilgrims travelled from?

   b Can you spot three words that Chaucer used that are still used today but spelt differently?

   c Can you spot any words that are still spelt the same today?

6 Read Source C. Was religion important to William of Lythwood? Give reasons for your answer.

+ Hungry for MORE

Look back at the map on the previous page. This shows the most popular destinations for medieval pilgrims. See if you can find out more about the miracles that are said to have taken place near you and the saints that performed them.

——— MISSION ACCOMPLISHED? ———

- Do you know what a medieval pilgrimage was and where they would visit?
- Could you explain to somebody two reasons why people chose to become pilgrims?
- Do you know how you could spot a pilgrim on the road and how they survived on the road?

What was life like in a medieval village?

MISSION OBJECTIVES

- To understand how most ordinary people lived during the Middle Ages.
- To know how a medieval village might have looked.

England was full of small villages in the Middle Ages. Most people lived in these villages and farmed the land. Most of the land was owned by the lord of the manor, who was usually a knight. The lord let the peasants live on the land in return for them obeying him and working for him three days a week.

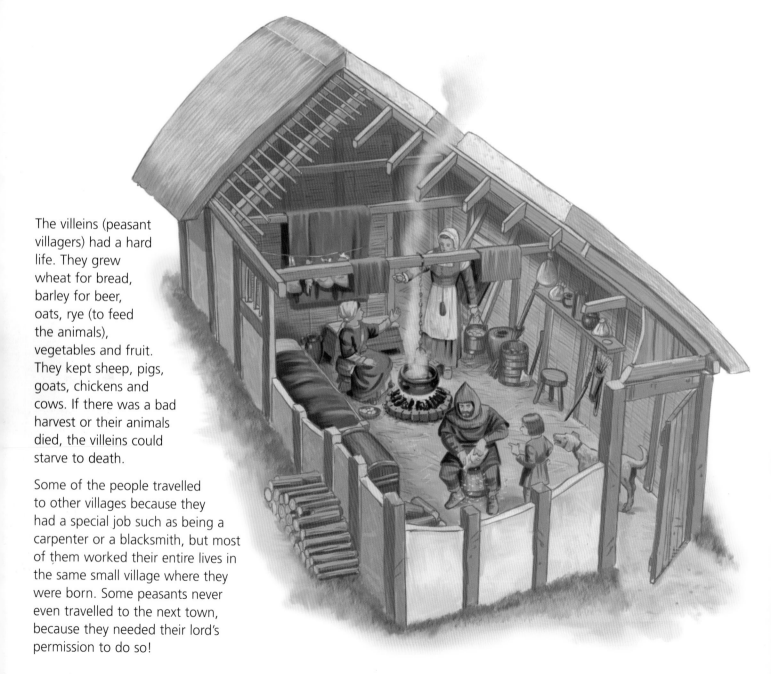

The villeins (peasant villagers) had a hard life. They grew wheat for bread, barley for beer, oats, rye (to feed the animals), vegetables and fruit. They kept sheep, pigs, goats, chickens and cows. If there was a bad harvest or their animals died, the villeins could starve to death.

Some of the people travelled to other villages because they had a special job such as being a carpenter or a blacksmith, but most of them worked their entire lives in the same small village where they were born. Some peasants never even travelled to the next town, because they needed their lord's permission to do so!

How does this villager spend his day?

He gets up when it's light enough to see and works all day. In the spring he ploughs the land and plants seeds. In the summer he harvests the hay, weeds the corn and scares the birds. In the autumn he harvests the corn and kills and salts some animals for winter. In the winter he clears any wasteland, repairs his hut and tools and, most importantly, tries to keep warm.

What about his wife?

She works as hard as he does. She cooks, cleans and looks after the children. She fetches water, makes and mends clothes and helps out in the fields when she is needed.

Where do they live?

In a one-room hut. The frame is made from wood and the walls are made from wattle (sticks woven together) and daub (mud, dung and straw). There are no windows and the floor is made of mud mixed with straw and ox blood to make it hard. There is a hole in the roof to let out the smoke from the fire inside. The animals live in the hut too... what a smell!

What do they eat?

- Breakfast – 6am. Bread and ale to drink (water wasn't safe).
- Lunch – 10am. Bread, perhaps an egg, a piece of fish or cheese. Ale to drink.
- Supper – 4pm. Bread and pottage (a thick vegetable soup). Ale to drink.

Couldn't the villeins just run away?

No, they weren't allowed to because the lord owned them. And if they did run off they could be tried in court and be punished. However, villeins were sometimes given their freedom by a kind or grateful lord – or they could buy their freedom if they saved up enough money!

❚❚ PAUSE for Thought

How many people do you usually see in one day? One hundred, three hundred, perhaps even more? You probably see more people in one day than a medieval villager saw in their whole life.

★ **WISE-UP Words**

daub
wattle

↵ SOURCE A: *A medieval farmer in action. An illustration from a medieval manuscript.*

❗ FACT Making a wall

What is **wattle** and **daub**?
The wattle is the framework of sticks and twigs woven together. The daub is the plaster (made from mud, animal dung and straw) that is smeared on top of this to make a wall.

'The poorest folk are our neighbours ... in their hovels, overburdened with children ... whatever they save by spinning they spend on rent, or on milk and oatmeal for food. And they themselves are often famished with hunger and wretched with the miseries of winter – cold, sleepless nights, when they get up to rock the cradle cramped in a corner, and rise before dawn to card and comb the wool, to wash and scrub and mend, and wind yarn and peel rushes for their rushlights ... while the Friars feast on roast venison, they have bread and thin ale, with perhaps a scrap of cold meat or stale fish ... I tell you, it would be a real charity to ... comfort these cottagers along with the blind and the lame.'

↰ SOURCE B: *The view of a medieval writer who wanted rich people to treat the villeins a bit better. From 'The Vision of Piers Plowman' by William Langland, 1390.*

Work

1 a Make a list of the kinds of food people ate in the Middle Ages.

b Write down three ways in which these foods are different from your meals today.

c In your opinion, who has the healthier diet? Give reasons for your answer.

2 Why did most people spend all of their lives in the same village?

3 Imagine you are a villein in a medieval village. Write a description of a day in your life. Here are some ideas to think about:

- How do you typically spend your day?
- What is your house like?
- Does your working day change throughout the year?
- Where will you work or visit?
- What sort of people will you meet?
- Is there a particular type of food you enjoy?
- At what times do you eat?

Woodland – only the lord can hunt in it

Church – most people go to church. Villeins have to give 10% of what they grow to the priest

Manor – home of the lord. Villeins work for him for 3 days a week

Mill – villeins have to pay to use it, and it was illegal to grind your corn yourself

River – villeins have to pay the lord to fish it

The **local castle** – it dominates the area

Open fields – divided into strips and each villein had one or two strips per field. One out of every three fields was left fallow each year

Villeins' huts – vegetables are grown in their own garden

The **village pub** – a mug of ale and a sing-song was a popular way to pass the time

Inn

Castle

Market day – a time to buy and sell goods... and be entertained by musicians, jugglers and dancing bears.

MISSION ACCOMPLISHED?

• Can you describe how a typical villager might spend his day in either spring, summer, autumn or winter?

• Can you identify five things you might find in villages all over England during the Middle Ages?

What was life like in a medieval town?

—————— MISSION OBJECTIVES ——————

- To understand what life was like in a medieval town and what a town might look like.
- To understand why towns grew.
- To understand how buying and selling was organised.

People who didn't live in the countryside, or in castles, lived in towns. When William conquered England in 1066 there were only about 15 towns with a population of more than 1000, and only about eight with more than 3000 living there. London was the largest with about 10 000 people, followed by Winchester and Norwich with about 3000 people each. Most people (about 90 per cent of the population) lived in small villages out in the countryside, with no more than 50 to 100 people living in them.

After 1066, towns began to grow. Sometimes they grew where major roads met or near a bridge where people came to buy and sell goods. Other towns grew near a castle or monastery. The local lord still owned these places, but, if the town continued to grow and the townspeople made lots of money, they might join together and buy their land and freedom from the lord or king.

This freedom, written down on a special piece of paper known as a charter, gave the townspeople the chance to run the town themselves. In fact, by 1400, about 300 towns had received their charter or freedom. By this time, London's population had grown to over 40 000.

WISE-UP Words

guild

1   Most streets were just dirt tracks.

2   A pedlar selling goods as he walks through the streets.

3   The Castle – at one time only the castle was here, but over the years the town built up in front of it.

4   Shops had picture signs to show what they sold because few people could read.

5   Large private house, probably the home of a merchant

6   Defensive tower and guardpoint.

7   Entrance gate – guarded by sentries 24 hours a day, seven days a week

8   Having fun – all sorts of people might entertain the townspeople in return for a few coins.

9   A young apprentice being taught the skills of a trade by a master craftsmen. The training lasted 7 years.

10 The market – held once or twice a week, people came in from the countryside to sell eggs, cheese, butter, fruit and vegetables.

11 Many houses had vegetable gardens

12 Market stalls – merchants brought in exotic goods from abroad such as spices and silks.

13 Meeting rooms above the gateway.

14 Traders bringing in goods by river.

15 A wagon bringing goods to sell at the market.

16 The Guildhall – where the town **Guild** met. This was a group of traders and craftsmen that made rules for its members to follow. They set prices, organised training and made sure goods were well made.

17 Town walls patrolled by guards.

↩ SOURCE A: *Market stalls around a town wall. Can you see what customers are buying?*

Town Charter

The king gives the officials running this town permission to:

1. **RENT LAND** for their own use without working for the lord

2. **HOLD MARKETS** every week without paying taxes to the lord

3. **HOLD FAYRES** every year

4. **FIX PRICES** for goods sold at market

5. **HOLD COURTS** to punish traders who break the rules of the market

6. **HAVE THE RIGHT OF GALLOWS** – to punish criminals by hanging

↑ SOURCE B: *A typical charter granted by a king or local lord in the Middle Ages.*

SOURCE C: *William Fitzstephen 'Description of the city of London' c1170.* ↴

'Traders can be found in their particular areas each morning. There is wine for sale on the river bank. Every day you may find food, dishes of meat – roast, fried and boiled; fish; cheap cuts of meat for the poor and more expensive for the rich. Just outside the town there is a field called Smithfield. On every sixth day of the week there is a sale of fine horses. In another part of the field are things brought to market by the country folk – farming tools, pigs, milk, cows, large oxen and woolly sheep, mares to pull the plough and young foals.'

wood	leather	fish	silk
grain	wine	hawks	soap
lead	farm animals	furs	canvas
spices	glass	rope	wool
salt			

↑ SOURCE D: *Goods for sale at Boston Fair in 1250. Some goods like wool, leather and fish, would have been produced locally. Other goods like furs, rope and wine would have been imported from abroad.*

WISE-UP Words

charter

Henry the lead beater
Robert the cook
Hugh the carpenter
Thomas the painter
Hugh the hosier
William the builder
William the butter maker
William the cutler
John the cordwainer
John the thatcher
Pagen the miller
Richard the combere
Robert the baker
William the belt maker
William the skinner
Richard the saddler
Edward the weaver

⤴ SOURCE E: *Craftsmen in Coventry in 1250*

Combere – prepared wool for
    clothmaking
Cordwainer – made boots
Cutler – made knives
Hosier – made stockings
Skinner – took skins off animals
Thatcher – made house roofs from
    straw or reeds
Weaver – made cloth

⤴ SOURCE F: *Medieval trades and their names.*

Poor workmanship will be punished by a fine
and having goods confiscated.
Shoemakers Guild, Chester

No one shall make or sell hats within the city
unless he has a burgess of the city.
Hatmakers Guild, London

If the threads of the cloth are too far apart,
the cloth and the tools used will be burned.
Weavers Guild, Bristol

If by chance a member of the guild shall
become poor through old age, accident or
sickness, then he shall have seven pence (3p)
from the guild every week.
Tanners Guild, (leather workers) London

⤴ SOURCE G: *Guild rules from a variety of towns.*

Work

1 List the main reasons why towns grew in certain places.

2 Look at the picture of a town on pages 62-63 and at Source A opposite. Imagine you live 10 miles away from town. For the first ever time, your parents are taking you into town, and it is the most exciting day of your life – new (and strange) sights, sounds and smells. Describe your visit.

3 Look at Source B.

   a What is a charter?

   b What advantages were there in having a charter for
   i the townspeople?
   ii the local lord or king?

4 Look at Source C.

   a Where in London would you have to buy
   i wine?
   ii sheep?

   b In larger towns (like London, Bristol and York), different parts of the town were used by traders selling the same thing. For example, all the silversmiths might be in Silver Street. What traders might you have expected to find in the following streets:

   Baker Street, Cutler Row, Pudding Lane, Gold Street, Brewhouse Lane, Vine Street and Tanners Lane?

   c What advantages might there be in having all the traders close together, for:
   i the buyer?
   ii the sellers?

5 Look at Source E.
   Copy and complete the following chart placing the name of the correct tradesman in each column.

Building trades	Making things to eat	Making things to wear	Other

6 **a** What was a guild?

   b Why do you think some of the guild rules were so strict?

   c Why do you think the guild chose to give money to their members who became poor because of old age, sickness or accident?

MISSION ACCOMPLISHED?

• Can you write five sentences that describe a typical town in medieval England?

• Do you know what is meant by the term 'charter' and 'guild'?

How smelly were the Middle Ages?

_____ MISSION OBJECTIVES _____

- To understand how and why standards of cleanliness and personal hygiene were very different from today.

We know today that dirt and rubbish are home to germs and disease. From an early age we are taught to avoid germs by washing hands regularly, clearing up rubbish, flushing toilets, brushing teeth and keeping ourselves clean. Our houses are full of cleaning products too; all designed to make our floors shinier, our clothes cleaner and our work surfaces germ-free! However, medieval people knew nothing of germs – not because they were stupid, they just didn't have the microscopes through which they could have seen them. As a result, people in the Middle Ages were a lot less fussy about living in smelly and dirty places than we are today. So just how smelly were the Middle Ages?

How clean is your castle?

Even rich people in their castles still lived a pretty smelly life. Only the very rich had a bath regularly, usually in a big wooden tub lined with cloth. Top quality soap made from olive oil and scented with herbs was available at a high price from abroad, but most soap was made locally from animal fat and wood ash. King John, for example, bathed once a month and was charged five pence by the man who organised it. This doesn't sound a lot but was the same amount that a labourer earned in a week!

Garderobes

A castle's toilets were little more than holes with stone or wooden seats. The lord usually had his own at the top of the castle, next to where he slept, and torn strips of cloth were used instead of toilet paper. Often the toilets, or **garderobes** as they were known, were built on different floors, one above the other. The sewage dropped down chutes straight into the moat (see Source A). Fish in the moat fed on the waste! If there was no moat, the sewage emptied into a pit, which had to be cleaned out by hand by the castle's gong farmer (see page 42)!

An ordinary peasant and his family were more concerned with having enough to eat than keeping clean. Their wooden cottages had no floorboards or carpets, just earth covered with straw. Windows – if they had one – were holes in the wall with a wooden shutter to keep out the wind. In the centre of the room was a fire, its smoke escaping through a hole in the roof. A medieval peasant must have always smelled of smoke – or even worse during the winter when they brought their animals inside and out of the cold! There were no taps to provide clean water for washing or drinking either; it had to be fetched from a stream, a river or a well. And there were no toilets, just a bucket in the corner of the room!

SOURCE A: _A diagram of how a castle toilet system might work._ ↱

'The floors are usually made of clay covered with straw. Under the straw is a mixture of beer, grease, bones, animal droppings and everything that is nasty.'

↳ **SOURCE B:** *A foreign visitor describing a cottage in the Middle Ages.*

'The butchers were often the worst. They used to throw out any waste and let the animals' blood run along the road. In hot weather, the smell was terrible. Townspeople still kept animals, which could be fed on the land around the town. But often they let their pigs roam around the streets, looking for food in the gutters. There were chickens too. And rats.'

↳ **SOURCE C:** *A modern historian writing about the sorry state of the streets.*

'Next case: the lane called Ebbegate. This was a right of way (a public footpath) until it was blocked by Thomas Wytte and William de Hockele. They built toilets which stuck out from the walls of their houses. From these toilets human dung falls onto the heads of passers-by.'

↳ **SOURCE D:** *Notes from a court case in 1321. Thomas Wytte, an owner of a house, and another man were taken to court because of their toilets. In another court case from 1347, two men were found guilty of piping their own sewage into their next door neighbour's cellar.*

A load of rubbish

In the towns, life was just as smelly. There was no organised collection of rubbish in medieval times. Instead, people just tipped their rubbish into the streets or dumped it into a pit and let it rot away. There were no drains or sewage pipes to carry away dirty water either. At night, people went to the loo in pots. The next day they tipped the waste out of the window into the street below! In London, there was a public toilet. It was located on London Bridge and emptied straight into the River Thames below!

Although houses didn't have bathrooms or running water, it would be wrong to think that all people were permanently filthy. Some towns had public 'bath houses' where you could have a wash for a small fee, for example, and a few places even employed **scavengers** to remove the filth. Some people also began to make the connection between rubbish and disease too. Although they didn't know about germs (they thought it was the bad smells from the rubbish that carried infection), it still led to England's first national Health Law in 1388 (see Source E).

'So much dung and filth and rubbish is thrown in ditches, rivers and other waters that the air is greatly infected and many illnesses and terrible diseases do daily happen. It is decreed, as well in London as in other cities and towns throughout England, that all they who throw dung, garbage, guts and other rubbish in ditches, rivers and other places shall have to remove, empty, or carry away, or pay to our Lord the King a fine of £20.'

↳ **SOURCE E:** *The Town Public Health Law, 1388.*

⭐ **WISE-UP** Words

disease
garderobes
germs
scavengers

! **FACT** What a job
Urine contains a chemical called ammonia which is used in the process of making leather. Old urine was collected from castles, towns and villages and sold to leather workers.

Work _____.

1 a Think about your own personal hygiene. What have you done over the last few days to keep yourself clean, tidy and as germ-free as possible? Make a list.

b Look at your list. Underline the things that people in medieval times would not have been able to do.

c Give reasons why people in the Middle Ages were not as clean as we are today.

2 Who were cleaner – the rich or the poor? Give reasons for your answer.

3 Imagine you have been asked to help inform a group of foreign visitors coming to medieval England. What can they expect to find 'when nature calls'? Explain about toilets in castles, towns and villages. You might like to consider:
- What toilet facilities would they expect to find in a castle?
- How did castle toilets differ from those out in the towns and villages?

___**MISSION ACCOMPLISHED?**___

- Can you explain where and how people in medieval times went to the toilet?
- Do you know how and why standards of cleanliness differed between rich and poor?

Could you have fun in the Middle Ages?

_____ MISSION OBJECTIVES _____

- To understand how both rich and poor spent their spare time in the Middle Ages.
- To understand some of the major differences between sport today and sport long ago.

In the Middle Ages, ordinary people didn't really have holidays. Instead, there were a number of feast days through the year, such as Easter Day, May Day, Midsummer's Eve, Christmas and various Saints' days. On these days, after going to a church service, they would be free to enjoy themselves. In fact, our word 'holiday' comes from the word 'holy day'. And people generally made their own fun too, using homemade equipment with whatever they had to hand. Some of the sports and games were so popular that they are still enjoyed today.

So how did ordinary people enjoy their holy days?

Bowling
Players would take it in turns to knock down as many skittles as they could with three balls.

Conkers
Became popular after 1066. The rules were simple – find a horse chestnut (or conker), drill a hole in it and thread it onto a piece of string. Then, taking turns, try and smash your opponent's conker to bits.

Mob football
No rules, no referee and as many players as you can get. Whole villages would play each other, with the goals several miles apart.

Ice skating
People would strap sharpened bones to their feet to use as skates. Archaeologists have recently found a skeleton of a young boy with his skates still strapped on his feet.
Thin ice perhaps?

Shin hacking
Two villagers would kick each other as hard as they could in the shins until one of them couldn't take the pain and gave up.

Golf
Using a few basic clubs, players would hit a leather ball stuffed with hair. Popular in Scotland and Holland by 1500.

Cold hand
A player would be blindfolded in front of a crowd and slapped by one of them. He or she would have to guess who hit them – and if they guessed correctly, it would be the 'slapper's' turn to be blindfolded. This was sometimes called 'blind man's buff' or 'hot cockles'.

Cock fighting
Two birds attacked each other, sometimes with metal tied to their claws. People would bet on the result.

What about the rich?

A rich noble may have gone to a tournament. This was a chance to take part in mock battles on horses and challenge another man to joust. He might go hunting in his forest, or stay in his manor house or castle to enjoy feasting or dancing. A group of acrobats or jugglers might entertain his guests. If the party got bored with the entertainers, they might play chess, draughts, cards, or throw dice.

In the Middle Ages a popular game for rich men was real tennis. Two players had to hit a wooden ball over a rope with a racquet. Sometimes the ball was hit so hard that players were killed by a ball hitting them on the head!

Do it yourself...

Whether you were rich or poor, you had to make your own fun in the Middle Ages. There were no cinemas or theatres to visit. You couldn't even go to an organised, professional sports match. But people must have enjoyed their spare time because they didn't get much of it. Holy days were rare, so ordinary people made sure that they made the most of them.

Archery
England's armies always needed archers. Boys had to practise from a very young age.

Stoolball
A young lady would sit on a stool and men would throw a ball at her. She would try to dodge the ball, perhaps using a bat to hit it away. If they hit her they got a kiss!

Bear baiting
A bear would be chained to a post while dogs attacked it. People would bet on the result – would the dog or the bear win?

Wrestling
People loved all sorts of fighting games – the more blood the better.

‖ PAUSE for Thought

Have you enjoyed any of the games or sports shown in the picture recently? If so, which ones? Have any of the sports or games changed at all? If so, how?

Work

1 Explain where the modern word 'holiday' comes from.

2 **a** Look closely at the illustration showing ordinary people enjoying their holy day. Make two lists, one headed 'Things we no longer enjoy today' and the other headed 'Things we still enjoy today'.

  b Choose one example from your list of things we no longer enjoy today. Explain why you think this pastime is no longer practised.

  c Choose one example from your list of things we still enjoy today. Explain in what ways, if any, it has changed since medieval times.

3 Design a poster to advertise a medieval holy day in your town. Make sure you include the name of the holy day, a programme of events and fun activities taking place. Add some illustrations. Remember, all holy days began with a church service.

——MISSION ACCOMPLISHED?——

• Do you know the origins of the word 'holiday' and how some people spent their holidays in the Middle Ages?

Has football changed much since the Middle Ages?

MISSION OBJECTIVES
- To identify the origin of football.
- To understand how football in the Middle Ages differs from football today.

About 1000 years ago, a small army from Denmark landed on the English coast and tried to steal as much as they could before sailing away again. However, their leader was captured and the angry English mob chopped off his head. The men then split into two groups and kicked the severed head around amongst each other. And so football was born.

The game soon became known as 'mob football' when all the men from the village played another. They usually met up once or twice a year on public holidays such as Shrove Tuesday (Pancake Day). It was very violent. There could be as many as 500 players, with few rules, no referee and the goals several miles apart. In Workington, an old rulebook said that players could use any method to get the ball to its target 'except murder'! The ball was a pig's bladder, stuffed with dried peas or sawdust. Sometimes a game was played with several balls!

SOURCE A: *A more modern view of football in the Middle Ages. A monk once described it as 'a devilish pastime. More a bloody murdering practice than a sport.'*

✚ Hungry for MORE
'Mob football' is still played in some parts of Britain today. Try to find out a bit more about this sport. Where is it played? Who plays it? How often? What are the rules? How do the players score?

'After lunch all the youth of the city go out into the fields to take part in the ball game. The students of each school have their own ball. The workers from each city craft also carry balls. Older citizens, fathers and wealthy men come on horseback to watch the juniors competing, and to revive their own youth. You can see their inner passions aroused as they watch the action and get caught up in the fun.'

SOURCE B: *The first description of mob football played in London on Shrove Tuesday, written by William Fitzstephen in 1174.*

Football was regularly banned. In 1314, the Mayor of London banned it: 'The hustling over large footballs causes great uproar in the city.' Despite the threat of imprisonment for anyone continuing to play, the ban was ignored! In 1331, King Edward III became the first king to officially ban football. He said that people were playing it so much they were forgetting to practise their archery skills. The king was worried that if a foreign army invaded England, men would have forgotten how to use their bows and arrows properly.

Indeed, football was one of England's most banned games. Between 1314 and 1667, it was officially banned by more than 30 royal or local laws. Richard II, Henry IV and Henry V all tried to ban it, but people were so determined to play that they carried on regardless. In Scotland, King James I once famously ruled that 'na man play a fute-ball', but the Scots loved the game so much they were playing football in Edinburgh the very next week.

SOURCE C: *A modern game of football. Can you spot any differences with mob football of the past?*

FACT Women's football
In the late 1400s, in the town of Inveresk in Scotland, a group of married and unmarried women started to play each other every few months. The married women regularly won. Women's football is not as new as some people would like to think.

FACT A dangerous game
In 1321 the Pope issued a special letter of forgiveness to a player who had accidentally killed an opponent. A few days later a Londoner wrote that players used to 'retire home as from battle, with bloody heads, bones broken and out of joint and bruises that will shorten their days'. By 1450 players in some towns introduced a new rule to try to reduce the number of accidents: the ball could only be kicked, not carried or thrown.

Work

1 Write these statements in the correct chronological order.
   • Women's football played regularly in Inveresk, Scotland.
   • A new rule was introduced in some towns saying the ball could only be kicked, not picked up.
   • King Edward III was the first king to ban football.
   • A Danish prince had his head used as a ball.
   • The Pope issued a special letter to forgive a player who had killed an opponent.

2 Which of the above events do you think had the biggest effect on the game of football? Explain your answer.

3 a Make a list of all the differences you can find between football in the Middle Ages and football today.

   b What do you think the biggest difference is? Explain your answer.

4 a Why do you think so many kings tried to ban football?

   b Why do you think the bans weren't very successful?

MISSION ACCOMPLISHED?

• Can you identify five differences between medieval and modern football?

71

The sound of music

• To understand how and why standards of cleanliness and personal hygiene were very different from today.

The Middle Ages had its own pop songs and dance music. There weren't any music channels (as there was no television) or pop charts, but listening to a live band – and dancing around – were still very, very popular in medieval times. So what was medieval music like? Who performed this music? And what other types of entertainment were popular?

Organ Tambourine Clarinet Viol Flute Drum Hurdy Gurdy Lute Trumpet

⤺ SOURCE A: *Common instruments for the Middle Ages. Since there was no way of recording, all music was sung 'live'.*

Music and dance

There were two types of music – 'sacred' (played in the church) and 'house' (played in and around people's homes). Church music had no harmonies, just a single singer singing a tune – and not one you'd spend the rest of the day humming! The music played outside church was much livelier. A band consisting of anything up to a dozen people would play all sorts of high tempo music on lots of different instruments (see Source A). People danced in large circles moving around clapping, spinning and jumping in time to the beat. Singing over a mug of ale outside your house or on the village green was a very popular pastime.

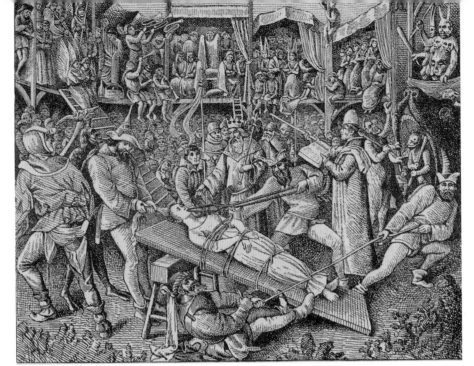

WISE-UP Words

miracle play
wandering minstrel

↵ **SOURCE B:** *Plays were common in midland and northern towns such as Wakefield and Chester. They are sometimes called miracle plays.*

Cymbal

Harp

Wandering minstrels

Singers known as 'minstrels' wandered from town to town entertaining the crowds. They sometimes sang for the lord in his castle, if invited, but generally played out on the streets so people could dance and sing along. They would usually expect a few coins in return for their performance. However, the minstrels weren't just popular for their singing – often the news they brought from other parts of the country was just as interesting as the show. After all, wandering around so much meant that they knew all the gossip from the local towns and villages!

Play time

Plays were another popular form of live entertainment and drew large crowds. Originally, they were put on in church to teach peasants about the Bible or about saints. Over time, they became morality tales where good overcame evil and were so popular they were moved outside.

Work

1 **a** What is the difference between 'sacred' and 'house' music?

b Which do you think was the more popular? Give reasons for your answer.

2 Look at Source A.

a List which instruments you have heard of before – or even played?

b Why was all music played 'live' in the Middle Ages?

3 **a** What was a 'wandering minstrel'?

b Apart from entertaining the crowds with music, what other role did wandering minstrels perform?

4 Look at Source B.

a What was a 'miracle play'?

MISSION ACCOMPLISHED?

• Can you explain what sort of music ordinary people enjoyed in the Middle Ages?

• Can you explain what a 'wandering minstrel' or a 'miracle play' was?

Keeping in fashion

MISSION OBJECTIVES

• To understand the role fashion played in the lives of the rich and how fashion changed during the Middle Ages.

To many people today, fashion is very important. You only have to look in any newsagent's to see dozens of fashion magazines, and whole satellite channels are dedicated to following the latest fashions. Most of you reading this page right now will be aware of the newest trends in shoes, hairstyles and jewellery.

Fashion was important in the Middle Ages too. The rich dressed in fancy clothes to impress each other. Clothes became a status symbol, with lords and ladies trying to outdo each other by wearing the latest costumes made from fine wool, linen, velvet, silk or fur. They decorated these clothes with gold and silver thread, jewels, chains and fancy buttons. Even the coloured cloth used to make the clothes had different meanings: blue meant you were in love, yellow meant anger and grey meant sadness.

FEMALE FASHION
Women's dresses were always long and got brighter and more elaborate throughout the Middle Ages.

late Saxon   1300s   1400s

HATS

Women often hid their hair beneath fancy hats, some shaped like animal horns or butterfly wings. The famous 'steeple hat', which was cone shaped and very fashionable in the late 1480s, was nearly a metre tall.

1300 ⟶ 1350 ⟶ 1400 ⟶ 1400

1400 ⟶ 1420 ⟶ 1450 ⟶ 1480

In the early Middle Ages, the rich wore fairly simple clothes – but as the years passed, fashions became more and more elaborate. Dresses got longer, hats got taller, cloth got brighter and shoes got pointier. And just like today, hats, shoes, hairstyles, coats, dresses and cloaks varied from year to year, so it was a constant fight for the most dedicated followers of fashion to keep ahead.

However, it was a very different story for the ordinary peasants. Following the latest fashions meant nothing to them. Instead they wore plain and simple tunics, woollen leggings, straw or woollen hats, hoods and capes. They dressed in dull colours such as grey, brown, dark green. Some peasants couldn't even afford to buy shoes. Their clothes were nearly always handmade and would last for years!

MALE FASHION

A well-dressed nobleman might wear a tunic, leggings and a hat, but throughout the Middle Ages the style of hat, length of tunic, thickness of robes and tightness of leggings would vary.

1100 ⟶ 1350 ⟶ 1470

SHOES

Pointed shoes called 'poulaines' were very fashionable in the Middle Ages. In fact, some shoes were so pointed that the toes had to be tied back. And platform shoes called 'patterns' were common too, for walking through the filthy, muddy streets.

PEASANTS' CLOTHES

Peasant's clothes were made from coarse wool or linen. They dressed practically rather than fashionably. In winter they kept warm by wearing leather or sheepskin jackets.

Work.

1 a Why was fashion so important to rich people in the Middle Ages?

b How could the clothes a person wore express how they might be feeling?

c In your own words explain how and why a poor person's clothes differed from a rich person's.

2 We all know that there were no fashion magazines in medieval England, but imagine that there were! Imagine you are an editor for a fashion magazine during the Middle Ages. You need to prepare a double page spread for a magazine bought by the rich and fashionable. Your feature could include the following:

- Latest fashions.
- Fashion dos and don'ts.
- What the best dressed people are wearing.
- The key points about the fashions, for example how pointed your hat should be.
- A 'headline' or spread title – this needs to be catchy and encourage the reader to do more than glance at your article.
- Examples of fashion styles.
- Bright, clear, colourful pictures.
- A layout like a magazine – look at examples in current magazines to help you.

MISSION ACCOMPLISHED?

- Can you explain three key differences between the clothing of the rich and the clothing worn by peasants during the Middle Ages?

The story of the English language

_____ MISSION OBJECTIVES _____
• To understand the origins of the language we speak.

What is the official language of England? English, of course. But did you know that for many years after 1066, it was the third most important language in England! So how did the English language survive? Why had it become less important after 1066? What did English sound like during this time? And how did English develop and become the number one language in England by the end of the Middle Ages?

Before 1066...

Before William the Conqueror and his men invaded (and took over) in 1066, the people of England spoke a language called Old English. This was a mixture of different languages taken from the various peoples who invaded England over the years. Source A explains the various influences in Old English.

SOURCE A:

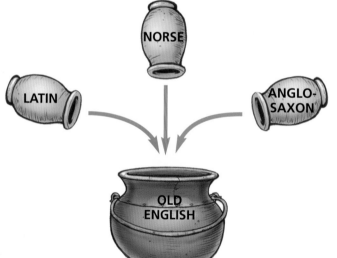

NORSE: From the 700s onwards, the Vikings attacked and settled in England. These 'norse men', as they were sometimes called, added some of their own words to the language. Many of the words they introduced were connected with place names, such as 'by' which is norse for a town. As a result, we get Grimsby and Whitby. Sometimes the Vikings settled in a village, and norse for a village is 'thorpe', so we get Scunthorpe and Cleethorpes. Other Viking or norse words include neck, flit, you, ugly, bull, gate, skin, anger, glitter, oaf and dregs.

LATIN: When Britain became a Christian country, a number of Latin words (mainly connected with the Church) came into use in England. Some of these words which still survive today are bishop, church, monk and baptism. Other Latin words or phrases such as factor, alter ego, parent and etcetera (although we write 'etc' today) are still used frequently.

ANGLO-SAXON: Tribes called Angles, Saxons and Jutes from Germany and Denmark invaded England about 1500 years ago. The Anglo-Saxons were great storytellers. The language they spoke would be difficult for us to understand but some of their words still survive. Indeed if you could travel back in time and speak to an Anglo-Saxon you would really struggle to know what he was talking about, but you might be able to understand some words such as was, name, silly, wife, drink, the, love, son, father and ground.

After 1066...

In 1066, William the conqueror brought the French language to England and King Harold, the man he had killed at Hastings, was the last Old English-speaking king! All the important people William brought over from France spoke French – the king himself, the queen, the barons, their wives and their children. They brought new words with them too – words that we still know today, such as battle, baron, enemy, castle, army, arrest, archer, judge, traitor, prison, guard, market, city, sausage, grape, sugar and plate.

The ruling class of England (and their lawyers, priests and secretaries) could also speak Latin – a living language in 1066. Latin was taught in schools and cathedrals and spoken by educated people all over Europe. After the Norman Invasion, Old English was officially the third most important language in England. Nobody wrote English down any more and nobody seemed to care! Kings and their friends spoke French (and Latin); churchmen, teachers and merchants used Latin, and books were even written in Latin too.

English only survived among the villeins and poor townspeople. The words they used and the way they spoke varied from place to place. Because different languages were used by different people, the result is still seen today, for instance objects for which there are two completely different words – one from Old English, the other from the French. The ordinary English peasant, for example, would use Old English words when looking after his animals – words such as ox, sheep, pig and calf. However, the rich Norman rulers, who ate these animals in their castles or manor houses would call them beef, mutton, pork and veal (in French: boeuf, mouton, porc and veau).

In the mix

As the centuries passed, Old English and French began to mix (just as the people did). An Old English-speaking peasant who knew a worker up at the castle might use a French word; a rich nobleman visiting the local town would also use a French word. He then might visit another town, pick up a few Old English words and use them with his friends. As the years passed, the two languages began to merge. Latin was still the language of the Church but in trade, business and in the growing towns and villages, it was awkward to have two languages, so they gradually blended into one. By the 1400s, something very similar to modern English had emerged.

SOURCE C:

The English language continues to absorb words from all over the world. Look below at just a few everyday words from other languages.

Arabic	admiral; sofa; alcohol
Japanese	tycoon; sushi; judo
Inuit (Eskimo)	igloo; anorak; kayak
Turkish	coffee; yoghurt
Czech	robot; pistol
Welsh	corgi; flannel
Portuguese	marmalade; albatross; palaver
Norwegian	ski; slalom
Hungarian	coach; paprika; goulash
Scottish Gaelic	slogan; trousers
Aztec	chilli; tomato; chocolate
Russian	vodka; mammoth

Work

1 a In your own words, explain what is meant by the term 'Old English'?

b Why did French replace Old England's official language in the Middle Ages?

2 Why do you think English eventually replaced French and Latin?

3 Look at Source B. According to this source, how was Chaucer helped by the variety of languages which had been used in England over the years?

4 a The English language is always changing. Think carefully and write down why you think the English language changes so much.

b Make a list of the words and phrases used today which your great-grandparents wouldn't understand. Try to explain why they wouldn't understand them.

'Chaucer has often been referred to as the 'saviour of the English language'. As a writer of the famous 'Canterbury Tales', he wrote mainly in English, the language of ordinary people, but used French words when he didn't think an English one fitted. For example, instead of using the word 'hard' (Old English) he may choose the word 'difficult' (French) instead. He thought his writing was improved by the richness of the English language. To put it simply, he had so many words to choose from – Old English, French, Latin, Norse and Anglo-Saxon.'

SOURCE B: *From a modern history book about Chaucer, a famous writer from the Middle Ages.*

! FACT Changing the language
William the Conqueror, William II, Henry I, Stephen, Henry II, Richard I, John, Henry III, Edward I and Edward II all spoke French as their first language. Many of these kings couldn't read or write either! It was Edward III who realised that English, not French or Latin, was still spoken by millions of ordinary people and so allowed English to be used in Parliament and in law courts. Soon after, Henry IV became the first monarch in over 300 years to make his first speech as a king in English.

MISSION ACCOMPLISHED?

• Can you name two Anglo-Saxon, two Latin, two French and two Viking words?

Ready, steady, cook

• To understand how food and drink in medieval England is totally different from the food and drink we enjoy today.

Think about what you have eaten over the last week. You may find that you've eaten chocolate bars, a few burgers or pizzas, chicken nuggets or maybe something more healthy such as pasta, rice or fruit and vegetables grown locally or imported from abroad. Today, we have more choice in where we get all our food, what we eat, even how we cook it, than ever before. Things have certainly changed a lot since the Middle Ages. So what was it like to eat in medieval Britain?

It ain't pleasant for a peasant

A peasant's food was pretty dull and the same year in year out. There was no tea, coffee, orange juice or fizzy pop and the water wasn't usually fit to drink so they drank a watery kind of beer called **ale**.

A peasant's basic food was tough black bread known as **rye bread** made from grain. This bread accompanied all meals. The first meal of the day was breakfast, eaten as soon as the sun rose. For dinner, taken about 10.00am, a peasant would again eat bread, along with cheese, onion, eggs and perhaps a jug of cider or ale. For supper, at about 4.00pm, the bread would probably be dipped in soup or stew (known as pottage) flavoured with vegetables, nettles, flour, dumplings and garlic.

⤶ SOURCE A: *The diet of a typical villager in 1300.*

Healthy diet

Peasants grew a lot of strong-flavoured vegetables and herbs to make their dull food tastier. Onions, garlic, leeks, cabbage, carrots (which were white not orange), parsley and mint were common. Apples, cherries, pears and wild berries were also eaten, and there might even be a few beehives because honey was one of the few ways to sweeten anything. In fact, a peasant's diet was probably healthier than that of a rich noble living in a manor house or castle, because they ate so many vegetables – the nobles ate lots and lots more meat!

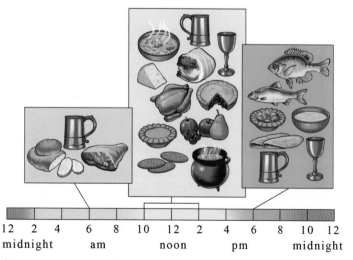

12	2	4	6	8	10	12	2	4	6	8	10	12
midnight		am				noon			pm			midnight

⤶ SOURCE B: *Lord's meal diagram.*

▌▌ PAUSE for Thought
Even today we still have a taste for salty or smoked food. For example, some of you will put extra salt on your chips or enjoy 'smokey bacon' crisps or 'smoked' kippers. We like these things because humans have been preserving food like this for thousands of years and our taste buds haven't changed much in that time.

▌ FACT Spud free zone!
Potatoes didn't reach England until the 1500s so there would be no chips or potato wedges for the peasants to enjoy!

What about the meat?

If peasants did eat meat, it was usually bacon. This was the most common meat amongst peasants because pigs, who tend to eat anything, were very easy to keep. But there were no refrigerators to keep food fresh so meat was usually salted or smoked. Peasants would spend days rubbing salt into meat to stop it going bad, or hang their strips of meat high up in the roof of their cottage so it would dry out and last longer.

Life in the manor house

For the richer folk, daily life was a lot easier than for the peasant. They had servants to do most things for them, including the cooking! They still ate a lot of bread, but it was a better quality wheat bread. Like a peasant, a rich noble would eat three times a day, but would eat a lot more meat – and drink a lot more wine! Soups and stews were common but occasionally there might be a pudding, perhaps a fruit tart or a pancake.

Medieval feast

For a special occasion, the lord and lady of the manor would hold a feast in their largest room – the great hall. A servant would lay out spoons, knives, drinking cups and bread. Forks were rare. The lord and his guests would probably have spent the day hunting for the meat about to be eaten – venison, wild boar, pheasant, crane, wild duck, swans or even peacocks. Slices of stale bread called **trenchers** were used as plates. The juices from the meat and vegetables would soak into them and when the meal was over they might be given to the poor – or thrown to the dogs (see Source C). Servants would then carry around warm bowls of water and bits of cloth so that guests could rinse and clean their fingers after eating.

A spicy story

Because people grew bored with salted and smoked food, sometimes spices were added to it to make it more interesting. But spices were so expensive (they had to be imported from abroad) that they were only for the rich. In castles and manor houses, spices were even kept in a locked cupboard.

⤶ **SOURCE C:** *A medieval feast.*

★ **WISE-UP** Words

ale
rye bread
trenchers

Work

1 Copy out and complete this paragraph, choosing one answer from the bold words in the brackets.

A peasant's basic food was (**bread/potatoes**) which he ate with all meals. Cheese, eggs and fish were popular too. They drank (**lemonade/ale**) with most meals because the (**water/whiskey**) was not fit to drink. Peasants often had a small (**garden/garage**) next to their cottage where they grew lots of strong-flavoured (**herbs/ vegetables**) and herbs to make their duller food a bit (**duller/ tastier**). (**Bacon/Lamb**) was one of the most common meats because (**dogs/pigs**) were so easy to keep. To preserve food over the long winter months, meat and fish were (**frozen/salted/ tinned**) and smoked.

2 a Copy out the diagram of a rich noble's meals (Source B).

   b Now draw a similar diagram to show your meals during one of the days during the last week. Remember to include everything you have eaten, even snacks.

   c Write down at least two ways in which the noble's meals are different from your meals.

___MISSION ACCOMPLISHED?___

- Can you explain what a trencher and pottage were?
- Can you explain how and why a rich person's food differed from a poor person's?

Knight life

MISSION OBJECTIVES

• To understand the importance and role of the knight in medieval society and how aspects of medieval history still have relevance today.

Have you ever kicked a football out of play because your opponent is injured? Or have you given up your seat on a bus for an elderly person or pregnant woman? Have you ever held a door open for someone, or, if you are male, allowed a lady to go through the door before you? If the answer to any of these questions is 'yes', you have probably been told what good manners you have. The person you've helped knows you didn't have to do any of these things, but they (and you) feel much better for doing them. So why do we do this? Where does this sort of behaviour come from?

From the Middle Ages?

Lots of sports today include these ideas about behaving properly and being courteous. For example, when playing golf or snooker, there are no rules to stop you making a noise when your opponent is taking a shot. However, players are quiet when their opponent is playing because they don't want to be seen as unsporting. But this idea of behaving in the correct manner has been passed down to us from the Middle Ages. And it all started with the best warriors in Europe – the knights.

The knight's code

The first knights were just soldiers on horseback. William the Conqueror brought them to England in 1066 to fight King Harold. As a reward for beating him, King William gave them land. In return, they promised to spend 40 days a year fighting for their king. This was called **paying homage**. From the twelfth century onwards, though, knights were expected to follow a strict code of honour, called **chivalry**. Inspired by Christian teachings, chivalry demanded that knights were kind, truthful, loyal, polite and brave in battle. They had to spend money and choose friends wisely, never break a promise and defend people who couldn't defend themselves.

The 'Code of Chivalry' also stated that the knights had to treat women especially well. They should fight for her, do brave things for her, write her poems and even be prepared to die for her. Even today, when a man helps out a woman in an extra special or kind way, it is often said that 'he was like a knight in shining armour!'. Indeed, this whole idea of behaving in the correct manner still survives; the next time someone thanks you for giving up your seat for them or holding open a door, just say, 'It's OK, I'm just being chivalrous!'.

Becoming a knight

If you wanted to be a knight, having a rich father helped. Being a knight was expensive because you had to pay for all your horses, weapons and men – and you were expected to give expensive gifts to your friends. You were supposed to come from a noble family too, although some people lied about their family history!

A knight's training would start at seven years of age when he would be sent to a knight's home to serve him. The **page**, as the boy would be known, would clean dishes, serve meals and wash clothes and might learn to read and write. At about 14 years old, the page would become a squire. He would learn about chivalry, weapons, fighting, armour and horses. And if the squire worked hard enough for another seven years, he might be ready to become a full knight.

Re-enactments of medieval tournaments are a popular tourist attraction, and regularly take place at castles in Britain during the summer holidays.

Knight life

Knights were given land by a lord in return for 40 days' military service a year. They spent time at the lord's castle and at their own manor house, probably a few miles from the castle. When they weren't guarding the lord, or fighting for him, they tried to make money in tournaments.

WISE-UP Words

chivalry
page
paying homage

A knight at last!

1: The young squire has waited years for this. He has learned all there is to know about being a knight, and now his time has arrived!

2: The night before, he has a bath to wash away his sins.

3: Then he spends the night in church praying. He promises to be a good worthy knight. The white tunic shows he is pure; the red robe means he is prepared to spill blood for his king.

4: Helped by the page and another squire, he puts on all his armour ready for the knighting ceremony.

5: The squire kneels before his lord or even the king and promises to be loyal and brave and to protect the poor and the weak. He is then 'dubbed' (touched) on each shoulder with the flat of his own sword.

Arise!

6: A knight is born! He is often presented with a set of spurs (used to control a horse), another sword and a new suit of armour. He will also visit the chapel so the priest will bless him so he should always triumph in battle.

Welcome to the tournament

If there wasn't a war to keep a knight fit and his skills sharp, the next best thing was a tournament. This was a mixture between a mock battle and a fun day out. And it gave a knight the chance to become rich and win some prizes too.

A medieval tournament – this was a chance for a knight to take part in all sorts of different competitions.

1 Tents for visiting knights.

2 An archery competition taking place.

3 The tournament marshal. He was like a referee making sure that everyone followed the rules and didn't cheat.

4 A beaten knight trying to buy back the horse he lost for falling off his horse during the joust.

5 The herald. His job is to announce the names of the knights in each contest.

6 The coats of arms of each knight taking part in the tournament.

7 A sword fighting competition. Not all knights jousted, some preferred other tournament games.

8 The ale tent.

9 A poor beggar, hoping that some of the crowd will take pity on him and throw him a few wins.

10 Entertainers performing for the crowd.

11 Stand for spectators.

12 The local lord and lady who were hosting the tournament.

13 Dog fighting – people would bet on the result.

14 A joust taking place. This was a contest between the knights on horseback. They would ride at each other and try to hit their opponent with a three metre long lance. Three points were awarded if he knocked his opponent off his horse, two points if he lost his helmet and one point if they hit any other part of his body. A point would be lost if he hit the horse. Also, if a knight fell off his horse, the opponent got to keep his armour and his horse.

19 A charging knight on horseback.

20 Lance – these weren't sharp because the knights weren't trying to kill each other.

21 Knights waiting to joust.

22 Horses were protected with armour and padding.

23 Grandstand for the richest and most important guests.

15 Winner's prize. Often this was a golden cup or a silver plate, but sometimes the prizes were rather unusual – in London in 1216 the prize was a huge brown bear! Some knights made a living out of jousting, taking part in tournaments all over Europe.

16 An injured knight.

17 A dancing bear.

18 The tilt. This barrier was introduced to stop the knight who has been knocked off his horse being trapped to death by his opponent's horse.

What was heraldry?

Once a knight put on his armour, he looked the same as any other knight. So, in order to stand out when jousting in tournaments, or to avoid being killed by his own men during battle, the knight decorated his shield. The designs could be made up of special pictures, patterns or colours. This special design was known as a coat-of-arms. Sometimes the knight would also wear a tunic or carry a flag with the same design as his shield. A coat-of-arms was a knight's personal badge and had to be easy to recognise. After all, during battle it was vital to know instantly who was coming towards you so you knew which side he was on. As the years went by, the patterns became very complicated and there were complex rules, called heraldry, for their creation.

Rules of heraldry

When designing their coat-of-arms, a knight had to follow several strict rules. To begin with, a knight was only allowed to use five basic colours – purple, blue, red, black and green. They were also allowed to use two metal colours – gold or silver. A knight then had to choose a simple design (see Source A).

There were even strict rules when selecting the colours for your pattern. For example, you couldn't put a metal next to a metal or a colour next to a colour (see Source B).

SOURCE A: *A selection of basic patterns each with their own name.* ↱

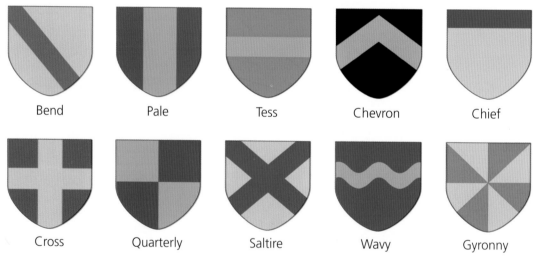

Bend   Pale   Tess   Chevron   Chief

Cross   Quarterly   Saltire   Wavy   Gyronny

! FACT

If a knight was captured in battle he would rarely get killed because he was valuable and his family would pay a ransom to get him freed. Captured knights were treated with great respect – another example of chivalry. When Edward, the Black Prince, defeated King John of France in 1356, he served food to the captured king at the victory feast. The Black Prince said it was a great honour to serve such a brilliant warrior.

SOURCE B: *Colour rules for a knight's coat-of-arms.* ↴

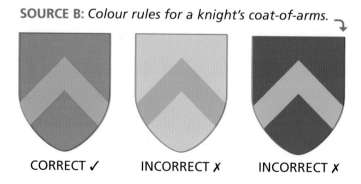

CORRECT ✓   INCORRECT ✗   INCORRECT ✗

Choosing your charge

A coat-of-arms often had a 'charge', an image that represented something about the knight or his family (see below).

strength and protection	safety and trust	strength and alertness	faithfulness	courage	a good judge
wisdom	ready for anything	bravery	beauty	truthful	affectionate

Family matters

Coats-of-arms were passed down through the generations and became family badges. They were plastered over everything – walls, gates, flags, clothes, windows, even plates and cutlery. When the members of two important families married, the two coats of arms were joined, and if they had children, special symbols were used which indicated where in the family they ranked (see Source C).

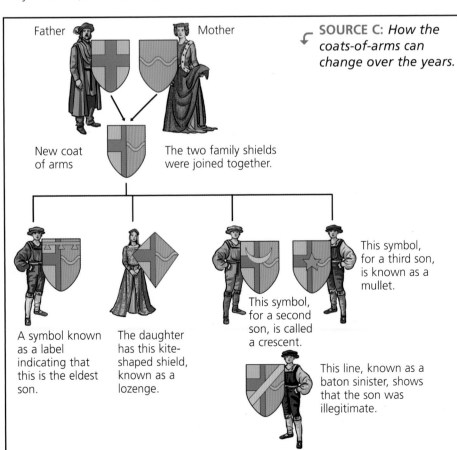

Father   Mother

SOURCE C: *How the coats-of-arms can change over the years.*

New coat of arms

The two family shields were joined together.

A symbol known as a label indicating that this is the eldest son.

The daughter has this kite-shaped shield, known as a lozenge.

This symbol, for a second son, is called a crescent.

This symbol, for a third son, is known as a mullet.

This line, known as a baton sinister, shows that the son was illegitimate.

FACT A herald
A herald was a man who knew all about this heraldry. He worked for the king or a baron. During a battle he would carry messages between the two armies and afterwards he had the horrible job of working out who the dead were by looking at their coats-of-arms.

SOURCE D: *A knight in coat-of-arms.*

Armour

A suit of armour could cost up to £75,000 in today's money. Most suits looked the same, so knights painted their own family's coat-of-arms on their shield to make sure they could be recognised in battle. Some knights even attached something on top of their helmet. Sir William Sidney attached a large silver porcupine to the top of his!

MISSION ACCOMPLISHED?

- Can you explain the following key words: 'chivalry', 'jousting' and 'heraldry'?

HOW TOLERANT WERE PEOPLE IN THE MIDDLE AGES?

Before starting this Historical Enquiry, you need to know what the word 'tolerant' means. Take a few minutes to discuss it with your class. You might find a dictionary useful here. In today's world, being tolerant of others is seen as a positive thing. A good citizen will tolerate other people regardless of age, sex, religion or skin colour. So, what were attitudes like long ago? Were people treated the same if they followed another religion, or were female, or looked different? Indeed, how tolerant were the Middle Ages?

1: Why were the Jews abused?

MISSION OBJECTIVES
- To understand how the Jews were different from the rest of the medieval English population.
- To know why the medieval English Jews were so successful.
- To decide whether England in the Middle Ages was a tolerant place.

The Middle Ages saw an ethnic minority move to England for the very first time. They were called Jews and followed a different religion, spoke a different language and looked unlike everybody else. So what made them move to England? How did they cope with life in a foreign land? And were they treated with tolerance in England?

A history of hate

The Jewish people have a long history of suffering and experiencing **intolerance**. They were thrown out of their homeland in the Middle East by the Romans in 153CE and were scattered throughout Europe in small communities. It wasn't easy being an outsider and Jews, who followed a different religion and were different in appearance, were often blamed whenever anything went wrong – and punished severely.

The first English Jews

It was the Norman Invasion in 1066 that first brought Jews to England. During the Middle Ages, the Church banned Christians from lending money to make a profit – but there were plenty of Christians who were desperate to **borrow** some! Jews don't believe that Jesus was the son of God and therefore don't live by the rules laid down by the Pope. This meant that medieval Jews were free to **lend** people money – and charge a fee for it. William the Conqueror brought them over because he thought they would be very useful to him when it came to improving the nation.

The profit of money lending

The first Jews that came to England were banned from all businesses apart from money lending. They were protected by the king in doing this and anyone found guilty of harming a Jew would be charged with damaging the king's property. They soon found plenty of people to lend money to. One Jew, Aaron of Lincoln was very successful and lent money to hundreds of people. These people included the King of Scotland, the Archbishop of Canterbury and lots of ordinary people. His money helped build cathedrals, abbeys and nine monasteries. He was not on his own; there were Jewish money lenders, including many women, in every major town in the land and they became a vital source of much-needed cash.

The pain of money lending

People hated having to pay their debts back – especially to wealthy 'outsiders'. The Jews soon became scapegoats whenever anything went wrong.

Royal disapproval

The Jews relied on the protection of the king for survival. In 1272, Edward I became king and that protection came to an end.

He passed a law that banned Jews from making a profit from money lending. As they were banned from any other jobs, many chose to leave the country.

Those that remained had to wear a yellow patch of cloth on their clothes so people knew they were Jewish.

Soon after that, worshipping God in the Jewish way was made illegal – even in their own homes.

Eventually, Edward gave all Jews until 1 November 1290 to get out of the country – on pain of death. It would be another 350 years before Jewish communities came back.

ALL JEWS MUST BE OUT OF ENGLAND BY 1ST NOVEMBER 1290
by order of the King!

! FACT

Jews made money from lending to people by charging interest. This means that the amount of money owed increases the longer it stays unpaid. In the Middle Ages, loans increased by four per cent a week!

WISE-UP Words

borrow
intolerance
lend

'When the Jews of York were massacred in 1190, among the first thing to be destroyed was the list of debts they held. It is possible that the hatred was driven by money rather than race.'

⤷ **SOURCE A:** *From 'Bloody Foreigners' by Robert Winder (Abacus) 2004.*

'One of the boats paid to take the Jews away struck a sandbar. The captain told his passengers to get off the boat and stretch their legs. He then sailed gleefully off the mud-flat, shouting that the Jews should seek help from Moses. Maybe they tried. But no one came to their aid. The sea did not part. They all drowned.'

⤷ **SOURCE B:** *From 'Bloody Foreigners' by Robert Winder (Abacus) 2004.*

Work

1 Name one way in which Jews were different from the rest of society in medieval England.

2 Explain why William the Conqueror brought the Jews to England.

3 a Read Source A. Why were the Jews in York attacked? Explain your answer.
   b Now read Source B. Why did the captain leave the Jews to drown? Explain your answer.

4 Was medieval England tolerant towards Jews? Write a paragraph explaining your answer, including as many reasons as you can.

MISSION ACCOMPLISHED?

• Could you tell someone two ways in which the Jews were different from the rest of the medieval English population?

• Have you decided whether medieval England was a tolerant place?

• Can you give two examples of intolerance towards Jews?

Throughout this book, you will read about the people who shaped the history of the Middle Ages. Often, it was a king or a baron or even a bishop. Rarely, the lives of ordinary peasants affected things and they are mentioned – but hardly ever women. What were the women up to? How were their lives different from women today? And, as half of the medieval population were female, why aren't they mentioned more often?

2: What about *her* story?

MISSION OBJECTIVES

- To understand the roles that women played in medieval society.
- To identify similarities and differences between the lives of women today and those from the Middle Ages.

In medieval England, women were seen as the possessions of men. In other words, they belonged to either their father or husband. If women got into trouble, it would be their closest male relative who appeared in court, not the woman herself. Most people at the time believed that women were **inferior** to men – both physically and mentally. Even the Church ruled that wives should be servants to their husbands! If a man felt that his wife was nagging too much or he thought she was getting too big for her boots, he could legally put her in a **scold's bridle** (see Source A). The bad news for women didn't end there; they were banned from lots of things we would now take for granted.

SOURCE A:
A scold's bridle. An iron muzzle or cage, the bridle had an iron curb which was pushed into the wearer's mouth making talking difficult or actually painful. ↱

A Woman cannot:
- *marry without her parents' permission;*
- *own property, clothes or jewellery – it belongs to her husband;*
- *divorce her husband – even if he beats her;*
- *train to be a doctor, lawyer, priest or judge;*
- *go to a shop, inn or travel on her own;*
- *wear tight or revealing clothes;*
- *speak rudely.*

The missing message of the monks

A lot of the information we have about the Middle Ages comes from monks. They were one of the few groups that could read or write – and they didn't have a great deal to do with women! They wrote about things that interested them, such as religion, rulers and fights between countries. Women didn't have a great deal to do with these things and most monks had no contact with women, so they were hardly mentioned.

Peasant women

Ordinary women's lives were tough. Their only education came from their mothers and they learned how to cook, sew and care for children and animals. The average age for girls to marry was 17, although some brides were as young as 13! A girl wouldn't have chosen her husband – her family would have done it for her. The husband would receive a **dowry**, a payment from his new wife's family, when he got married.

Village women

If the woman lived in the countryside, she would either work in the fields or make cloth at home. As well as working all day, she was expected to cook all the food and care for the young children!

↳ SOURCE B: *A woman's job was to look after the babies and make sure food was prepared.*

Town women

It was possible for women to learn a trade in some of the bigger towns. The most common jobs for women were spinning and weaving cloth – unmarried women are still called spinsters today. Many women ran businesses but only after their husbands had died. Women couldn't start their own firms but they could inherit one.

Rich women

Wealthy women had time for fun, which would usually involve dancing and music. Although they received less education than rich men, women were expected to run the family household and manage the servants.

WISE-UP Words

dowry
inferior
scold's bridle

↳ SOURCE C: *A picture of hardworking women drawn in about 1250.*

Work

1 List as many examples as you can of medieval society being intolerant to women.

2 What had to happen before a woman could become successful in business?

3 Writing in full sentences and using capital letters and full stops, explain why historians don't know as much about the lives of women in the Middle Ages.

4 If you had to choose, which would you rather be: a peasant woman, village woman, town woman or rich woman? Give reasons for your answer.

5 List as many ways as you can in which you think the lives of women have improved.

_____ MISSION ACCOMPLISHED? _____

• Do you know what rights medieval women had?

• Could you explain to somebody what kinds of jobs women did in the Middle Ages?

• Have you spotted what has changed in women's lives since the Middle Ages?

↳ SOURCE D: *This medieval picture shows women fighting. Although there weren't female soldiers, women helped defend castles in seiges when things got desperate.*

Having seen how women were treated during the Middle Ages, it may not surprise you to learn that between 1066 and 1553 there were no female monarchs in England. Women were viewed as being too weak to rule a whole country. In 1135, all that nearly changed when Princess Matilda was named as heir to the throne. So why wasn't Matilda crowned queen? Who gained control of the country instead? How did she react? And who would have made the better ruler?

3: Matilda: England's forgotten queen

MISSION OBJECTIVES

- To understand why Matilda thought she should have been crowned queen in 1135.
- To understand the reasons why she wasn't.
- To decide who won out of the struggle between Stephen and Matilda.

Henry's got no heir!

In 1120, King Henry I was the father of two sons and two daughters and certain that the English crown would remain in his family's hands after his death. Then disaster struck! Both of his sons drowned coming back from France. It is said that after Henry heard the news, he never smiled again. He was still desperate to ensure that the Crown remained in his family. Before he died he made the barons swear to make his daughter, Matilda, queen after he was gone. But the thought of having a woman in charge was too much for many barons. When Henry died, they broke their promise, and looked to his nephew Stephen. Look at the Fact files of the contenders to the throne!

MATILDA

Background: She married a German King when she was 12 years old and lived in Germany for ten years until her husband died in 1125. Henry I soon found another husband for her – and 24 year old Matilda married a 14-year old French Prince! Despite the difference in ages and rumours that they didn't get on, the couple had three sons in four years.

Claim to the throne: She was the eldest child of Henry I and was her father's choice as heir. The barons had sworn to make her queen.

Personality: She grew up in Germany and didn't seem to like England much. She could be rude and arrogant and didn't make friends easily.

STEPHEN

Background: His father had been killed fighting abroad when Stephen was just five years old. He was brought up by his uncle, Henry I, and soon became a great favourite of the king. He was given huge amounts of land by Henry and by the time the king died, Stephen was the richest man in England.

Claim to the throne: Despite swearing to support his cousin Matilda, Stephen didn't think a woman was capable of controlling England. As he was Henry's closest male relative, Stephen decided that the Crown should be his!

Personality: He was very mild-mannered and good tempered. He was sometimes accused of being too laid back and indecisive.

When Henry died in 1135 Stephen raced back to London. He was crowned king with the support of the barons and the Church before Matilda could act. Stephen was a weak king and the barons started to abuse their power. The country descended into chaos as the people were taxed into starvation.

Matilda was not going to give up the throne without a fight. With the country going to ruin, some barons started to give their support to Matilda and a civil war began. After four years of fighting, Matilda's army captured Stephen. The Crown was hers and she declared herself 'Lady of the English'.

Just when it looked as if she had victory, Matilda threw it all away! Her stuck-up attitude made her very unpopular with the people of London. They rose up in revolt and chased her out of town – all the way to France! With Matilda out of the way, weak-willed Stephen was free to become king again.

Matilda still didn't give up and after more years of fighting, a compromise was reached in 1154. Matilda agreed to stop opposing Stephen if he agreed to name her son as heir to the throne. When Stephen died in 1154 it wasn't his son Eustace who took over but Matilda's son Henry II.

'In the days of this king (Stephen), there was nothing but strife, evil and robbery, for quickly the great men rose against him. Every powerful man built himself castles and held them against the king. When the traitors saw that Stephen was a good humoured, kindly man who inflicted no punishment, they committed all manner of horrible crimes. It grew worse and worse. They took tax, as protection money, from villages. When the wretched people had no more to give, they robbed and burned all the villages.'

⤆ SOURCE A: *A description of the way the barons took control under Stephen.*

"
Matilda sent for the richest men and demanded from them a huge sum of money, not with gentleness but with the voice of authority. They complained they did not have any money left. When the people said this, Matilda, with a very grim look, every trace of a woman's gentleness removed from her face, blazed into unbearable fury.
"

⤆ SOURCE B: *A description of Matilda written when she was in control of the country.*

Work

1 Who do you think should have been made the English monarch in 1135? Give reasons for your answers.

2 Find as many reasons as you can to explain why Matilda wasn't made queen.

3 Were any of them good enough reasons to keep her off the throne? Give reasons for your answer.

4 Read Source A. Why do think that people saw Stephen as a poor king?

5 Read Source B. Do you think Matilda would have made a better ruler than Stephen? Explain your answer.

___ MISSION ACCOMPLISHED? ___

• Do you know why Matilda expected to be made queen?

• Could you explain why Stephen became king?

• Have you decided who won this battle of the sexes?

The people of medieval Europe all had one thing in common – Christianity. Apart from the Jews, everybody followed the Pope as their religious leader. But the holiest place on earth for Christians wasn't in Europe, it was Jerusalem in the Middle East. The area where Jesus had lived and died was known as the Holy Land and it was a favourite destination for pilgrims. The Holy Land had been controlled by Muslims since 638CE, but Christians were free to come and go as they pleased. In 1095, the Pope told the people of Europe to leave their families and fight for control of Jerusalem. So what had changed? And how did they get all the way to the Holy Land to fight in the Crusades?

4: What were the Wars of the Cross?

MISSION OBJECTIVES

- To understand why the people of medieval Europe were interested in the Middle East.
- To know why Jerusalem was an important city for Christians, Muslims and Jews.
- To understand why the Pope ordered the Crusades.

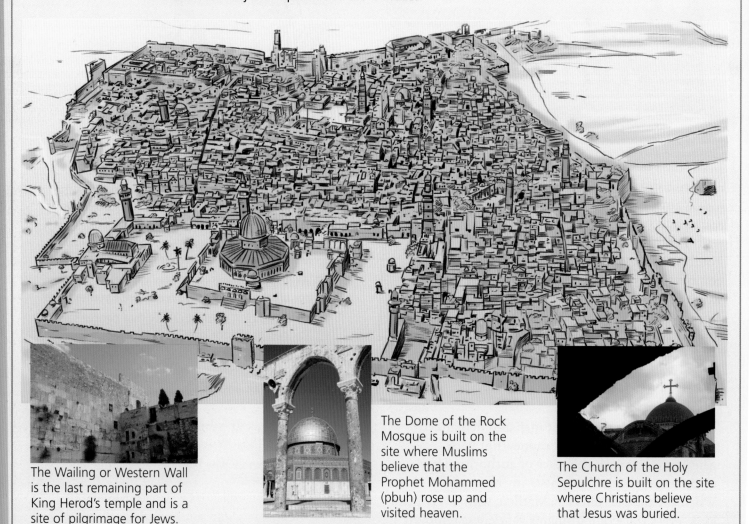

The Wailing or Western Wall is the last remaining part of King Herod's temple and is a site of pilgrimage for Jews.

The Dome of the Rock Mosque is built on the site where Muslims believe that the Prophet Mohammed (pbuh) rose up and visited heaven.

The Church of the Holy Sepulchre is built on the site where Christians believe that Jesus was buried.

⤶ SOURCE A: *Jerusalem was a sacred city for three different faiths. As you can imagine, members of all three religions wanted safe access to their shrines. It is because of this that people still struggle for control of Jerusalem to this day.*

Who ruled Jerusalem?

Jerusalem was taken over by an Egyptian Muslim leader, in 638. He gave Jews and Christians freedom to worship and thought that tolerance would make people respect Islam. Other leaders that followed were not always as tolerant but Christians and Jews continued to be allowed to visit and live in Jerusalem. In 1079, all that changed. Another Muslim group from Turkey seized control of the city. The Turks had a different opinion from the Egyptians when it came to other religions. They didn't see why these non-believers should be allowed into the Holy Land. Christians and Jews began to be attacked. The Pope became very concerned. His people were being stopped from visiting the land of Jesus, but the Turks were also invading other lands that belonged to Christians. He decided something had to be done.

'There is an urgent task which belongs both to you and God. You must hasten to carry aid to your brothers living in the East, for the Turks have attacked them and have advanced far into Roman territory. They have seized more and more of the lands of the Christians and have already defeated them seven times in many battles, killed or captured many people, destroyed churches and have devastated the Kingdom of God. If those who go lose their lives on the journey or in fighting, their sins will be absolved (forgiven) immediately. I grant this by the power God has given me. Let those who have fought wrongfully against others now rightfully fight the infidel, let those who have been robbers become soldiers of Christ.'

↳ **SOURCE B:** *Part of the speech made by Pope Urban II in 1095, the beginning of the Crusades.*

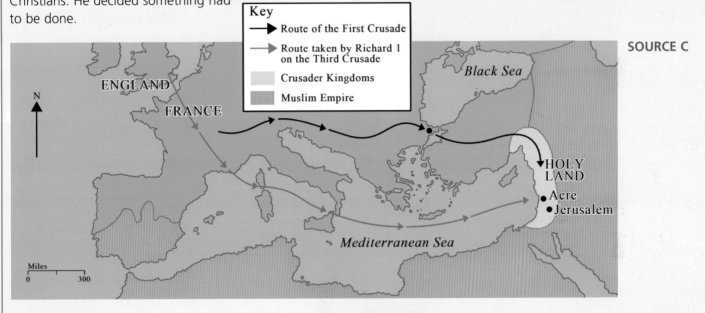

SOURCE C

Key
→ Route of the First Crusade
→ Route taken by Richard 1 on the Third Crusade
Crusader Kingdoms
Muslim Empire

Work

1 Explain why Jerusalem is an important city for:

a Muslims;

b Christians;

c Jews.

2 Write a paragraph explaining why you think Pope Urban III ordered the Crusades in 1095.

3 Read Source B. How did the Pope try to encourage people to go on the Crusades?

4 Design a poster for the Pope that would encourage people to leave their homes and fight on the Crusades. It must tell people why the Pope wants them to fight and what benefits are in it for them.

! FACT The word "crusade"

Today, the word 'crusade' is often used to describe a struggle against something that is bad. The police are often said to be on a crusade against drugs and Batman was known as the Caped Crusader after his fights with comic book villains. But the word crusade actually comes from the Latin word for cross. In the Middle Ages, the word was used to describe a struggle against enemies of the cross – the symbol of Christianity.

MISSION ACCOMPLISHED?

- Do you know why the people of medieval Europe were interested in the Middle East?
- What other religions believe Jerusalem is a special place?
- Could you explain why the Pope ordered Christians to go on a Crusade to the Holy Land?

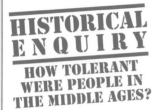

HISTORICAL ENQUIRY
HOW TOLERANT WERE PEOPLE IN THE MIDDLE AGES?

The age of the Crusades lasted for nearly 200 years. Time and time again, Christian armies set off from Europe to fight for control of Jerusalem. There were victories and defeats on both sides and, over the years, the Christians began to call their opponents 'Saracens', from the Greek word for Muslim. The Turks began to call the invaders 'Franks', as many of the Crusaders were from the Frankish area of Europe. So which Crusades were successful for the Franks? Which were won by the Saracens? And who was in control of the Holy Land when the Crusades ended?

5: The chronicles of the Crusades

―――――――――― MISSION OBJECTIVES ――――――――――
- To understand how long the age of the Crusades lasted.
- To know the key features and results of the main Crusades.
- To identify examples of tolerance and intolerance in the struggle for the Holy Land.

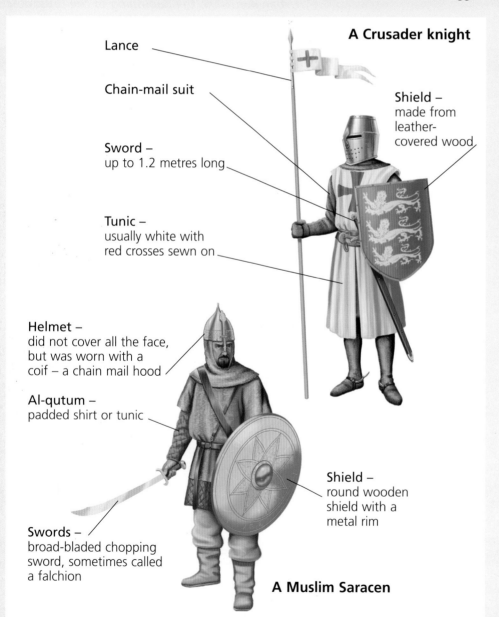

A Crusader knight

Lance

Chain-mail suit

Sword –
up to 1.2 metres long

Tunic –
usually white with
red crosses sewn on

Shield –
made from
leather-
covered wood

Helmet –
did not cover all the face,
but was worn with a
coif – a chain mail hood

Al-qutum –
padded shirt or tunic

Shield –
round wooden
shield with a
metal rim

Swords –
broad-bladed chopping
sword, sometimes called
a falchion

A Muslim Saracen

THE PEOPLE'S CRUSADE

Date: 1096

Leader: A French monk called Peter the Hermit.

Who took part? A few thousand peasants, including a few knights and women and children.

What happened? These were the first people to answer the Pope's call to go and fight the Turks. It was more of a rabble than an army and had few proper weapons and nowhere near enough supplies. After a long and hazardous journey, the people were slaughtered or sold into slavery.

Result: A crushing Muslim victory. The Holy Land remained in the hands of the Turks.

THE FIRST CRUSADE

Date: 1097

Leader: Robert of Normandy, son of William the Conqueror.

Who took part? Over 3000 noblemen and knights from Europe who were very well trained and armed. It was the first serious attempt to capture the Holy Land so, despite the earlier People's Crusade, it was known as the First Crusade.

What happened? It took two years and many battles for the Crusaders to reach their goal. The Christian knights managed to capture the cities of Nicea in 1097 and Antioch in 1098. The following year they reached the huge defensive city walls of Jerusalem.

The Battle of Jerusalem

Things didn't look good for the Franks when they reached the most important city of them all. The long journey, disease, baking heat and ferocious battles had taken their toll on them, with only about half their number actually reaching the battlefield. The Muslim tribes had been at war with each other – which made things easier for the Crusaders – but Jerusalem seemed too difficult to conquer. The Saracens had poisoned the water holes outside the city walls and the Christians were also fast running out of food.

They were saved by Italian supply ships and when their siege equipment arrived – the Franks attacked! Huge steel hooks were catapulted onto the city walls to try and pull them down, while enormous battering rams smashed into the gates. The defending Saracens threw pots of greek fire – an early form of bomb – over the walls at their attackers. After a month of fierce fighting Jerusalem finally fell to the Crusaders. Once inside the city, the Christians ran amok and murdered over 70,000 Muslims and Jews – including many women and children. Large parts of the city were set on fire and precious items from the Dome of the Rock Mosque were **looted**.

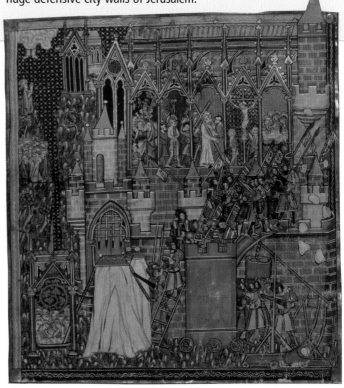

Once Jerusalem had fallen, the knights of the First Crusade swept through the Holy Land, creating Christian kingdoms and building castles on the captured land. Some Europeans decided to stay behind and make sure that the Holy Land remained in Christian hands.

Result: A Christian victory – the Crusader states of Antioch, Edessa, Jerusalem and Tripoli ruled over the Holy Land for the next 60 years.

The warrior monks

To protect the Christians who decided to stay in the new Crusader Kingdoms, two groups of warrior monks were founded. These holy orders were a mixture of monasteries and armies, but often ended up doing more fighting than praying. The Knights Hospitallers of St John of Jerusalem had been formed to care for sick pilgrims but soon turned into an elite fighting force. The Knights Templars were created to defend pilgrims from attack when they were in the Holy Land. Both groups became very successful, rich and powerful – too powerful for some people. The kings of Europe were unhappy that these warrior monks were free from their control and only had to answer to the Pope. Their wealth and secrecy made people very suspicious and the Knights Templars were **disbanded** in 1312.

⤴ **SOURCE B:** *This magnificent castle, Krak des Chevaliers, was built by the Crusaders in Syria in 1142 to make sure the land remained under Christian rule.*

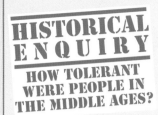
────── MISSION OBJECTIVES ──────

• To understand how long the age of the Crusades lasted.

• To know the key features and results of the main Crusades.

• To identify examples of tolerance and intolerance in the struggle for the Holy Land.

THE SECOND CRUSADE

Date: 1147

Leader: Emperor Conrad of Germany and King Louis VII of France.

Who took part? Up to 50 000 German and French knights. The Christian kingdom of Edessa had fallen to the Saracens in 1144 – the aim of the Second Crusade was to win it back!

What happened? The Franks were heavily defeated at Damascus.

Result: The Muslims continued to grow in strength and confidence. Many historians see this as a turning point in the Crusades. By 1174, the Saracens had united behind one leader – Salah ad-Din – known to the Franks as Saladin. By 1187, Jerusalem was again under Muslim control.

THE THIRD CRUSADE

Date: 1189

Leader: Richard I (the Lionheart), King of England. Philip of France and Emperor Frederick of Germany.

Who took part? The best knights of medieval Europe. The brilliant Muslim leader Saladin had recaptured Jerusalem. The Third Crusade's mission was to win it back!

What happened? Emperor Frederick drowned before he reached the fighting, but his men pickled his body and took it with them. The other leaders of the Crusade, Richard and Philip, spent most of their time either suffering from dysentery or arguing. They managed to capture the town of Acre, but Philip returned home soon after. Richard was **isolated** and he and his army were suffering from illness.

Despite victory against Saladin's forces at the Battle of Jaffa, Richard was unable to recapture Jerusalem. On 2 September 1192, he met with Saladin and worked out a deal. Jerusalem would remain in Saracen hands but Christians would be tolerated and allowed to visit there without coming to any harm.

Result: Historians can't agree. Richard won some famous victories and gained access to the Holy Land for Christians. Saladin made sure that Jerusalem had remained under Muslim control.

THE FOURTH CRUSADE

Date: 1198

Leader: Pope Innocent III

Who took part? The Pope decided that it was time that the Church took control of the Crusades. He was frustrated by the failure of the Third Crusade to capture Jerusalem. This time he didn't ask kings for help, he asked individual barons and cities instead. All sorts of people set out to find riches and adventure in the East.

What happened? The Crusade never even reached the Holy Land. Many of the Crusaders were more interested in making themselves rich than fighting for Christ. Rival Christian groups captured Constantinople but then fought against each other for control of the city.

Result: A disaster for the Christians. By fighting each other, they had weakened their forces and allowed the Saracens to expand their control. Never again would a Christian army set out to capture Jerusalem.

THE CHILDREN'S CRUSADE

Date: 1212

Leader: Stephen, a 12-year-old French shepherd boy.

Who took part? Stephen claimed he had been visited by Jesus and told to lead an army of children to rescue the Holy Land. He claimed that Jesus had told him that the sea would part and let them walk to Jerusalem. Some said that as many as 30 000 children flocked to join him. The youngsters were certain they would succeed where the adults had failed.

What happened? Towards the end of June, the army of children set off on the road to the port of Marseilles. The summer was unusually hot and the children relied on charity for survival. Many died on the journey and many more turned back for home. Those who reached Marseilles were devastated to see that the sea hadn't parted. Some turned against Stephen and left for home. Those that stayed, boarded ships that they were promised were sailing for the Holy Land. All of those on board were sold to the Saracens as slaves and never heard from again.

Result: A tragedy.

There were other Crusades than those listed here but the Christians were unable to repeat their early success. The great period of the Crusades finally came to an end in 1291 when the Saracens finally captured Acre, the last Frank city in the Holy Land. Every Christian in Acre was slaughtered. After nearly 200 years of trying, the Christian Crusaders had failed to take and keep control of the Holy Land.

! FACT

Saladin was the **Sultan** of Egypt and leader of the Muslim armies after 1176. He was a highly respected warrior and won many famous battles, both against the Crusaders and rival Muslim groups. For over 50 years, the Christians had built castles all through the Holy Land and they seemed safe from attack. By uniting all the Muslims, Saladin began to turn the tide. His victory at Hattin led to the recapture of 50 Crusader castles and, by 1189, the Holy City of Jerusalem was under Saladin's control. His amazing victories led to the launch of the Third Crusade and a showdown between Saladin and Richard the Lionheart.

He was feared and respected in equal measure. After the Battle of Hattin, he ordered the slaughter of all of the warrior monks and the bravest Frank soldiers. However, when he heard that Richard the Lionheart was suffering from illness, he sent him fruit and ice to cool him down. He also ordered that the Christians inside Jerusalem be saved from death after his forces had captured the city – so he could hold them to ransom! He also tolerated Christian worship inside the city after his deal with Richard.

Work

1 Put the following years in chronological order and explain what happened in each year.

1189 • 1097 • 1212 • 1096 • 1147 • 1198

2 Why do you think the First Crusade was a failure for the Christians?

3 Find an example of the Christian armies being intolerant and write a short description of it in your books.

4 Now do the same thing for the Muslim armies.

5 Look at the Fact box. Was Saladin a cruel or a tolerant man? Give reasons for your answer.

6 In no more than 150 words, explain which side you think won the Crusades. You must include examples of both Frank and Saracen victories and explain who controlled the Holy Land when the Crusades came to an end.

↵ **SOURCE C:** *A Saracen attack on the city of Jerusalem from the Hollywood film 'Kingdom of Heaven'.*

___ **MISSION ACCOMPLISHED?** ___

• Do you know how many years Christians and Muslims struggled for control of the Holy Land?

• Could you give an example of both the Christians and Muslims being intolerant?

• Could you give an example of someone from the Crusades being tolerant?

• Do you know who controlled the Holy Land when the Crusades came to an end?

The Crusades were a series of horrific battles and there were many atrocities committed by both sides. However there were also times when the Christians and Muslims mixed with each other and all sorts of ideas were exchanged. So what were these ideas? How did they affect life in Europe? Which were the most important? And do they prove that Muslims and Christians were tolerant of each other?

6: What can we learn from the Crusades?

MISSION OBJECTIVES

- To understand how life in Europe changed and improved after contact with the Muslim world.
- To decide which change was most important and why.

Before the Crusades

The Muslims had been in contact with Christians from Europe long before the Crusades began. They had conquered Spain in the seventh century and had traded with their Greek neighbours for centuries. But Christians from northern European countries like Germany, France and England had no contact with the Muslims. They had very little respect for the Saracens at first and thought they were a godless, backward people. They were in for a surprise! In times of truce, in between the Crusades, the two sides mixed. Without a doubt the Franks learned the most.

New products

Lots of things were brought back and became extremely popular. These included foods such as lemons, melons, apricots, sugar, syrup and spices like nutmeg and cinnamon. Cotton, silk and slippers changed the way people dressed and the lute changed the sound of European music. They also stole the idea of using pigeons to deliver messages from the Muslims!

Technology

The Muslims thought that studying and education were very important. Because of this, they had made advances in science and technology that amazed the Franks. These included mirrors, the magnetic compass, the magnifying glass and a tool that could measure the distance between stars called an **astrolabe**. The Muslims had also made advances in sailing the seas and improving surgical tools.

Knowledge

The Saracens used a number system that made complicated mathematics far easier, and arabic numbers are the ones we use today. The Saracens also had better maps and more advanced ways of measuring the land than the Franks. The works of the Ancient Greeks, which had been lost in Europe, had been translated by the Muslims. This meant that the ideas of Plato and Socrates could be re-discovered by the Europeans.

Warfare

The Saracens used archers a lot. European armies, especially the English, started to train men to use bows and arrows. They also took the Arab concentric castle design home with them and the giant siege machine called the trebuchet.

⭫ SOURCE A: *The Crusaders learnt the game of Shah, which they called chess, from the Muslims.*

Work

1 Look at the diagram of what the Europeans learned from the Crusades.
   a List all the things that they learned from fighting the Saracens.
   b Now list all the things that they learned from tolerating and talking to the Muslims.
   c Which list is longer – fighting or tolerating? Explain why you think this is.
   d Of all of the things that the Franks learned from the Crusades, which do you think was most important? Give reasons for your answer.

2 Look at Sources A to E. Divide your page into two. Label one side 'Tolerate'. Label the other 'Fight'. Write a brief description of each source under the heading that you think it belongs to.

'When I used to enter the Aqsa Mosque, which was occupied by the Templars who were my friends, the Templars would leave so that I might pray in it. One day I entered this Mosque, said Allah is great and stood up in the act of praying. Upon this one of the Franks rushed on me, got hold of me and turned my face eastward. 'This is the way thou should pray!' he said. A group of Templars seized him and repelled him from me. They apologised to me saying: 'This is a stranger who has only recently arrived from the land of the Franks. He has never before seen anyone praying except eastward'.'

⭫ SOURCE B: *From a book written in the twelfth century by Usama ibn Mundqidh, a rich Muslim from Damascus.*

'We who were Westerners find ourselves transformed into inhabitants of the East. The Italian or Frenchman of yesterday has become a Palestinian. We have already forgotten our native land. Some men have already taken Syrian women as wives. Races utterly unlike each other live together in trust.'

⭫ SOURCE C: *Written by a Frenchman, Fulcher of Chartres, in around 1120.*

" A man was accused of a crime, so they dropped him in water. Their idea was that if he was innocent he would sink, but if he was guilty he would float. This man did his best to sink but he could not do it. He was found guilty and they pierced his eyes with red hot metal – may Allah's curse be upon them. "

⭫ SOURCE D: *Usuma ibn Munqidh writing about the Christian's trial by ordeal.*

'These people study no science and are more like animals than human beings. Those who live in England are so far away from the sun that they have become stupid.'

⭫ SOURCE E: *A Muslim scholar's opinion of the Frank invaders.*

MISSION ACCOMPLISHED?

• Could you explain to someone how life in Europe changed after the Crusades?
• Have you decided which change was the most important and explained why?

Have you been learning? 2

TASK 1

A homophone is a word that sounds the same as another word but has a different spelling and meaning, for example a sale in a shop and a sail on a ship. Although they are pronounced the same, they are always spelt differently.

Copy the sentences below, writing the correct words from the choices in brackets.

a Young girls were taught to (sew/so) by their mothers.

b A monk would get up at (too/two) in the morning to (pray/prey).

c Christians and Muslims (fort/fought) each other during the Crusades.

d Most Crusades involved fighting in the (Wholly/Holy) Land.

e (Some/Sum) people treated Jews badly because they followed a different religion.

f Monks and nuns (wood/would) dedicate their lives to God.

g Much of the food they (eight/ate) in the Middle Ages would be horrible or boring to us.

h (Sum/Some) Crusaders travelled by land, others travelled by (see/sea) to reach Jerusalem.

TASK 2

A noun is a word used to name a person, animal, place, thing or idea. There are a number of different types of nouns.

Abstract nouns describe things that cannot be detected with the five senses. So they can't actually be seen, heard, smelt, touched or tasted. For example, 'power' and 'tolerance'.

Proper nouns always start with a capital letter because they describe a specific person, place or thing. For example, 'Jerusalem' and 'Saladin'.

Common nouns also describes a person, place or thing but only in a general way. For example, 'woman' and 'pilgrim'.

Collective nouns describe a group of things, animals or people. For example, 'team' and 'herd'.

Copy this table and sort the nouns into the correct columns. The first ones have been done for you.

Common nouns	Proper nouns	Abstract nouns	Collective nouns
soldier	King Richard I	betrayal	fleet

nuns • archers • town • castle • monk • monastery • France • Glastonbury • Holy Land • Scotland • Canterbury Cathedral • poverty • terror • religion • bravery • work • exhaustion • pair • swarm • pile • flock • squadron • sheaf

TASK 3

Note-making is an important skill for a historian. To do it successfully, you must pick out all the key words in the sentences. The key words are the words that are vital to the meaning of the sentence. Without these words, the sentence makes no sense.

For example, in the sentence 'The German Emperor Frederick died whilst travelling on the Third Crusade', the key words are Frederick, died, Third Crusade.

Write down the key words in the following sentences. These key words form your notes.

a Pope Urban II called on the Christians of Europe to travel to the Holy Land to fight Muslims in 1095.

b Jerusalem was a very important city to people who followed three different religions.

c The First Crusade was very successful for the Franks as they captured the Holy City of Jerusalem in 1099.

d The Second Crusade was very successful for the Saracens as they crushed the Christian armies in battle in 1147.

e There is evidence that the two sides tolerated each other because the Christian armies learnt many things from their Muslim opponents.

TASK 4

The following sentence doesn't make much sense. All of the commas have been taken out. Copy the passage out, placing commas where you think they are needed.

Football in the Middle Ages had very few rules only murder was banned! There was no limit on the amount of players that could take part no kits for the teams to wear no referee and no goal posts. The ball was made from a pig's bladder that was stuffed with sawdust dried peas and then sewn up. The game became so popular that it was banned in some places because it caused violence injuries damage to property and even death! Eventually new rules were introduced such as that the ball could only be kicked not carried or thrown.

TASK 5 Why did people go on Crusades?

In 1095 Pope Urban II made a passionate speech calling for all Christian kings, noble and knights to go on a religious crusade to regain Jerusalem from Muslim Turks whom he had heard were robbing and torturing Christian pilgrims travelling to the Holy Land.

There are actually five different versions of what the Pope really said, so it is difficult to know the exact words he used. However, there are enough similarities in the different accounts to give historians a general outline or 'best guess' as to what he said. Source A is one of the most popular versions of what he said. Source B shows Pope Urban II setting the knights off on the crusade.

Source A: *Urban II calling for the First Crusade, in France on 27th November 1095*

> 'Beloved brothers, I speak as a messenger to reveal to you God's will. We cannot refuse to give help we have promised to our brothers in the East. They now need it desperately ... I therefore urge and beg you who are the voices of Christ, both rich and poor, to drive the foul vermin from the lands where your Christian brothers live and to bring speedy help to the worshippers of Christ ... Promise your support without delay. Let the warriors get ready and find what they need to pay for the journey. When the spring comes let them leave in good spirit under the banner of the Lord.'

Source B

As soon as word of Urban's speech reached England, bishops and priests travelled the country urging people to join in this 'holy war'. They were very successful because all sorts of people, both rich and poor, signed up to fight in what became known as 'the Crusades'.

1 a Look at Urban's speech again. What different methods does the Pope cleverly use to get people to go on this Crusade? How does he try to convince people to go?

b Think carefully. Why do you think there are so many different versions of this speech? Why do you think it is so hard to establish what people REALLY said in the Middle Ages?

2 a Copy out all the reasons listed below why people went on the Crusades.
To obey Pope Urban II
To spread Christianity
To have an adventure
To visit the Holy land
To steal from the places they visited
To bring back new ideas and goods
To gain land in another country
To make friends and establish new contacts
To prove how brave they were
To earn freedom from their master by fighting for him

b Now look at the list of people below:

KING, KNIGHT, PEASANT, MERCHANT, PRIEST

Think about each character and write their name next to the most likely reasons for them going on a crusade. You may write their name next to more than one reason. For example, you would probably write 'priest' next to 'To obey Pope Urban II' but are highly unlikely to write 'priest' next to 'To steal from the places they visited'!!!!

c In your opinion, which was the most important reason (or reasons) why people went on crusades.

d Draw a recruiting poster called 'Christianity needs you!' which is aimed at trying to get as many people as possible on Urban's 'holy war'. What illustration will you choose to draw? How will you try to 'sell' the crusade? What part, or parts, of Urban's speech will you use?

3 Look at Source B. In your own words, carefully describe the scene in the picture.

We all know that medieval England was ruled by kings and queens – but they didn't always get their own way. Over the next few pages you are going to look at three different occasions when the king's power was tested. But who would dare argue with the king? What happened to them? And how have these power struggles affected British history?

1: The Crown versus the Church: Henry II and Thomas Becket

MISSION OBJECTIVES
- To understand why Henry and Thomas were friends and why they fell out.
- To understand what this meant for relations between the Crown and the Church and who won the power struggle!

King Henry II and Thomas Becket used to be good friends. They hunted, got drunk and chased women together. They both enjoyed expensive clothes, magnificent palaces and the very best food and wine. Henry respected and trusted Thomas so much that he made him **Chancellor**. This was a very important job and meant he was in charge of the country when Henry was away. Their friendship finally ended when one of them was brutally murdered and had the contents of his head splattered all over a cathedral floor! But how did such good and trusted friends become enemies? What made them fall out? And who paid the ultimate price?

Henry the hot head!
King Henry was a popular ruler but he did have one major fault – his temper. He liked to get his own way and, when he got angry, his eyes went bloodshot and he threw a massive tantrum. He once got so angry that he ripped all his clothes off, threw himself on the floor and started chewing the straw off it!

Henry's master plan!
Despite being king, Henry did not have the power to punish everyone in his kingdom. People who worked for the Church and broke the law went to the Church's own courts instead. You may not think this was much of a problem but, in 1162, one in six people worked for the Church in some way. Henry was worried that there was too much crime and he thought that the Church courts were too soft on law-breakers. For example, the king's courts might cut off the hands of a thief, but the Church's courts would probably send them away on a pilgrimage. Henry wanted a clever and trusted friend he could put in charge of the Church. That way, the Church's courts would punish people the way he wanted – and his power would be complete!

Archbishop Becket

Henry made his friend Thomas Becket the Archbishop of Canterbury, placing him in charge of religion in England. Unfortunately for the king, Becket took his new job very seriously indeed. He stopped getting drunk, chasing women and wearing fancy clothes. He started to wear an

itchy, goat-hair shirt and slept on the hard stone floor. Religion became very important to Becket and he spent hours every day praying. When Henry spoke to him about making changes to the Church and their courts, Becket refused. The two men began to argue, and after Henry lost his temper in one particularly nasty disagreement, Becket fled to France – for six years!

Guess who's Beck?

Becket returned because the country needed an Archbishop of Canterbury and Henry and Becket agreed to try and work together. But as soon as Becket returned to England it all kicked off again! All of the bishops that had helped Henry while Becket was away were **excommunicated**. This meant that they were sacked from their jobs, but more importantly, their souls would be sent straight to hell and tortured for all eternity! Henry was furious.

In one of his rages he shouted, 'Is there no one who will rid me of this turbulent priest?' Four knights were stood nearby while the king ranted and raved. They decided that they could rid their king of this priest. They set off to Canterbury without delay.

Work

1 Before the four knights set out to kill Becket, the following events occurred. Write these down in the correct chronological order.
   • Becket ran away to France for six years.
   • Henry and Becket became best friends.
   • Henry made Becket Archbishop of Canterbury.
   • Henry made Becket Chancellor of England.
   • Henry was heard to say: 'Is there no one who will rid me of this turbulent priest?'.
   • Becket excommunicated some bishops.

2 a Think of five adjectives to describe King Henry II.

   b Think of five adjectives to describe Thomas Becket.

   c Are any of your words the same? Using the words you have listed, write two paragraphs describing Henry and Becket.

3 Explain Henry's plan when he made Becket Archbishop of Canterbury. What went wrong with this plan?

___ MISSION ACCOMPLISHED? ___

• Could you describe Henry and Becket's relationship before Becket became an Archbishop?

• Can you explain how Becket changed after he got his new job?

• Do you know how and why this ruined Henry's master plan to increase his power?

The evening of the 29 December 1170 was a dark and stormy one. Four knights, in full battle armour, had arrived outside Canterbury Cathedral. Some monks, sensing trouble, hurried inside to find Archbishop Becket and rush him to safety. The events that followed caused a sensation throughout medieval Europe. If it had happened today, it would be a huge news story that would be covered by lots of television companies and journalists. If there had been TV news in 1170 (which there wasn't – obviously!) it may have been presented something like this…

2: Murder in the cathedral

MISSION OBJECTIVES

- To understand how Thomas Becket was murdered and by whom.
- To be aware of the consequences of the murder.

TV Reporter: Hello, you join me amid shocking scenes here at Canterbury Cathedral. I can confirm the news that Thomas Becket, the man in charge of religion in England, has been hacked to death inside the most important cathedral in the country. I can also exclusively reveal that the four men who have been officially linked with the murder are knights and were apparently acting under orders from King Henry! The knights, named as Reginald Fitzurse, William de Traci, Richard Britto and Hugh de Morville, have fled into the stormy night. But if it is confirmed that they are Henry's men, it will cause a shock that will reach all the way to the Pope in Rome.

TV Reporter: You join me now inside Canterbury Cathedral with Edward Grim, a monk who claims to have witnessed the whole incredible incident. What did you see Brother Edward?

Edward Grim (monk): It was truly awful, you'll have to forgive me – I'm still shaking with anger and fear. The murderers entered this house of God in full armour and with their swords drawn. Some of my brother monks had tried to bolt the doors to keep the knights out, but the Archbishop ordered them to be re-opened. He said, 'It's not right to make a fortress out of a house of prayer'.

In a crazed fury, one of the knights yelled out, 'Where is Thomas Becket, traitor to the king and country?'

Becket stood in front of his attackers and said, 'I am no traitor and I am ready to die.' The knights then grabbed hold of the Archbishop and tried to drag him outside in order to kill him. Becket clung to a pillar but, realising that his time on Earth was nearly over, he bowed his head in prayer and made his peace with God.

This was too much for the murderous knights and a sword was brought crashing down on Becket's head, nearly chopping my arm off as it passed. Then another sword slashed down, again at his head, but still Becket stood firm in his prayers.

The third blow was swung with such force that it knocked the Archbishop to his knees.

As he knelt prone on the floor, a fourth and final blow cut the top off his head – the sword of the murderer smashing to pieces on the cathedral floor with the force of the strike.

But these evil men weren't finished yet. One knight put his foot on the holy priest's neck and scattered his blood and brains all over the floor. I couldn't bear to look any more but Brother William said he saw one of them scooping Becket's brains out of his skull with his sword. The last thing I heard was one of the knights saying, 'Let us away, this fellow will get up no more!' With that, the murderers disappeared into the night.'

TV Reporter: Thank you Brother Grim, an amazing story there. People of Canterbury are already dipping rags in Becket's blood. King Henry II and The Pope are yet to release statements but we are standing by to get their reactions to the story of the century!

Although this TV report is imaginary, the events it describes are recorded in witness statements and other evidence available to historians. The people of England were indeed shocked by Becket's murder and wondered what was going to happen next.

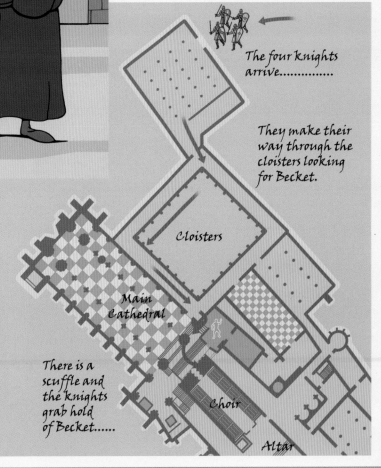

The four knights arrive...............

They make their way through the cloisters looking for Becket.

Cloisters

Main Cathedral

There is a scuffle and the knights grab hold of Becket......

Choir

Altar

❙❙ PAUSE for Thought
Why do you think the knights tried to drag Becket outside the cathedral?

⤴ SOURCE A: *Canterbury Cathedral.*

How did Henry II react?

Henry was horrified when he heard the news. He hadn't exactly ordered the knights to go to Canterbury but he knew he was going to get the blame. What terrified him most was being excommunicated by the Pope. He decided to say sorry – in a big way! Henry walked the streets of Canterbury with no shoes on and, when his feet were all cut and bleeding, he approached the Cathedral. He then prayed at Becket's tomb while monks whipped his bare back. He spent the night on the hard stone floor – on the very spot where Becket was killed. It worked, the Pope forgave Henry.

⤵ SOURCE B: *A medieval picture of murder.*

What happened to the knights?

The knights were not as fortunate as Henry. They were sent on a pilgrimage – all the way to the Holy Land. None of them survived the long journey there.

Saint Thomas Becket

People started claiming miracles were taking place at Becket's tomb as soon as he died. Blind people claimed they could see and deaf people claimed they could hear after visiting his tomb. In 1173, Becket was made a saint by the Pope and before long, the journey to pray at Becket's tomb was the most popular pilgrimage in England.

Work

1 Who do you think was to blame for Becket's death? Find one reason to blame:
- the knights;
- King Henry II;
- Becket himself.

Overall, who do you blame most for the murder? Was it a combination of some or all of them? Explain your answer.

2 Design a front page for a newspaper article reporting the events of 29 December 1170. Try to include the following details:
- An eye-catching headline (can you use alliteration?).
- Include the most important parts of the story in the first few sentences.
- Some quotes from an eye-witness.
- A picture of the crime scene.
- An interview with King Henry II.

3 Why do you think Henry reacted to Becket's murder the way he did?

4 Design a lead badge for pilgrims that visit Becket's tomb. Remember, it must have no words on it but must get the message across of where the pilgrim has been.

5 Who had the most power in medieval England – the Church or the Crown? Give reasons for your answer.

↰ SOURCE C: *Medieval woodcut of Henry II being whipped.*

___MISSION ACCOMPLISHED?___
- Could you tell somebody how Archbishop Thomas Becket met his death?
- Can you explain how Henry reacted?
- Have you decided who had more power in medieval England – the Crown or the Church?

The next power struggle didn't involve the Church, it was with the men who helped the king control the country – the barons! So which king faced the struggle? Why were the barons angry with him? And who won this tussle for power?

3: The Crown versus the State: The struggle against the barons

MISSION OBJECTIVES

- To understand what mistakes King John made that upset the barons.
- To know what the Magna Carta is and the effect it has on the world today.

King John – the Magna Carta man

King John was the son of Henry II and younger brother of Richard the Lionheart. He was unlucky because by the time he became king in 1199, his older brother had spent nearly all of the Crown's money fighting abroad. He didn't make things any easier for himself though – and he made mistakes that made many people turn against him.

MISTAKE NUMBER 1: He lost wars!

It's very difficult to lose wars and remain popular as king. Not only did John lose wars against the King of France, he lost all the land that his father had ruled, including Normandy. This earned John a new nickname – 'Lackland', because he lacked land. Others called him 'Softsword' because of his defeats in battle.

MISTAKE NUMBER 2: He upset the Pope!

John didn't learn from the mistakes his father made. He tried to increase his control over the Church and wanted to choose all of the bishops and archbishops himself. The Pope refused so John banned him from England! The Pope was so angry that he closed all of the Churches in the country for seven years. People believed that this meant that nobody could get christened, married or buried under the eyes of God. That made lots of people angry with King John.

MISTAKE NUMBER 3: He asked for high taxes!

King John demanded soldiers and money from his barons. They grew angrier and angrier – why should they give so much money and their best fighters to such a bad leader? John made things worse when he ordered that sons had to pay a tax when their fathers died. As you can imagine, this upset lots of people.

MISTAKE NUMBER 4: He was cruel!

John treated the monks very badly and once threw some blind and crippled monks out of a monastery. It was also rumoured that he murdered his nephew Arthur in a drunken rage. According to one monk, 'John became drunk and murdered him with his own hand and, tying a heavy stone to his body, threw it into a river.'

By 1215, patience was running out. The barons gave the king a choice: change the way the country was run or face a fight against the barons' armies.

The march to Runnymede

The barons came up with 63 clauses or rights that they thought all barons should have. This list of rights became known as the **Magna Carta**, which is Latin for 'Great Charter'. The king marched out to meet the barons' armies at a meadow near Runnymede in Surrey. Some of the barons thought it was a trap and fled the scene. It wasn't and King John sat down to **negotiate**. After days of discussions, the king agreed to the rights laid down in the Magna Carta. But he didn't sign it because he couldn't write! Instead, he sealed it with a blob of melted wax.

Magna Carta – the important bits!

I, King John, accept that I have to run my country according to the law. I agree:

Not to interfere with the Church

Not to imprison barons and nobles without trial

That trials will be held quickly and fairly

To stop unfair taxes

That I will not ask for extra taxes

To let merchants travel around the country to buy and sell without having to pay large taxes.

That might not seem such a big deal and, at the time, it was seen as a bit of a failure. But the Magna Carta grew more and more important as the years passed and it is now famous around the world. For the first time the law was written down that everybody had to live by. No longer could the king wake up in a bad mood and have a baron imprisoned or executed just because he felt like it. The law said that the baron had to have a trial. Power had been taken away from the king – and given to a piece of **parchment**!

The Magna Carta today

In 1215, the laws of the Magna Carta only protected barons and other nobles – they didn't apply to ordinary people. Today, the most important laws of the Magna Carta apply to everybody. For example:

- We have the right to a fair trial before we can be punished.
- We have the right to fair taxes.

WISE-UP Words

Magna Carta
negotiate
parchment

! FACT

In 1776, America copied part of our Magna Carta. When they wrote the constitution, they included: 'No person shall be held to answer for a crime without trial by jury nor shall their life, liberty or property be taken without following the law.'

Work

1 Imagine you are a baron in England in 1214. Write King John a letter explaining why you're angry with him. Make sure you tell him what angers you most and why. Remember to set it out like a proper letter with the address of your castle and the king's address at the Tower of London.

2 Write three sentences explaining why people still think that the Magna Carta is important today.

3 Create your own Magna Carta for your school. List at least six changes you would like to see. Remember, these rules must apply to everybody, students and staff, and they must improve your school or education. Explain your reasons for each rule.

MISSION ACCOMPLISHED?

- Can you tell someone the reasons why the barons rebelled against King John?
- Could you explain what 'Magna Carta' means?
- Do you know why it has affected the world today?

HISTORICAL ENQUIRY
WHO RULES?

King John died in 1216, just a year after he had agreed to the Magna Carta. His nine-year-old son Henry became King Henry III of England. The boy-king was helped by advisors to run the country and they promised the barons that they would stick to the laws of the Magna Carta. But Henry did not stay a boy forever. What did he do to fall out with the barons? How did the barons react to their new king's changes? And what did all this mean for the country?

4: The Crown versus the State: The struggle against the barons – a son's revenge?

―――――― **MISSION OBJECTIVES** ――――――

- To understand why Henry III became as unpopular as his father.
- To know how the barons reacted to Henry III's rule.
- To understand how this led to the first Parliament.

The young king comes of age

In 1234, Henry took over from his advisors and ran England by himself – and that's when all the problems started!

Mistake number 1!
Henry gave all of the best jobs to his friends! One of his mates, Peter des Riveaux, had the jobs of treasurer, keeper of the King's wardrobe, Lord Privy Seal and Sheriff of 21 counties – all at the same time!

Mistake number 2!
He lost wars! Henry tried to win back the land in France that his father had lost. Unfortunately, he wasn't a very good soldier and the wars were a disaster.

Mistake number 3!
His wife Eleanor! She begged Henry to make her uncle the Archbishop of Canterbury, even though he wasn't meant to interfere with the Church. The monks were not happy and Eleanor was once pelted with rubbish!

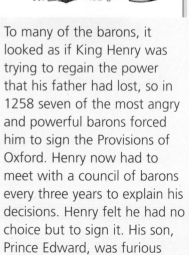

Mistake number 4!
He asked for high taxes! It wasn't just the failed wars in France that needed paying for. Henry was quite wasteful with money and even tried to buy the Italian island of Sicily for his young son Edmund.

Mistake number 5!
He wasn't very nice to people! It wasn't just the monks he upset. When his first son Prince Edward was born, Henry demanded that Londoners bring him expensive gifts to celebrate. He didn't say thank you, and even sent back gifts he didn't like!

To many of the barons, it looked as if King Henry was trying to regain the power that his father had lost, so in 1258 seven of the most angry and powerful barons forced him to sign the Provisions of Oxford. Henry now had to meet with a council of barons every three years to explain his decisions. Henry felt he had no choice but to sign it. His son, Prince Edward, was furious and swore revenge!

110

De Montfort in da house!

Young Prince Edward decided to confront the barons and personally led the king's army into battle at Lewes in Sussex. Unfortunately for Edward, the barons' army, led by Simon de Montfort, won the battle. Edward was taken prisoner as de Montfort saw his chance to reduce the king's power even more and, in 1265, he set up the first **Parliament**.

The word 'Parliament' comes from the French word 'parler', which means to talk. And that is exactly what happened at Parliament – the king talked about how best to run the country. De Montfort's Parliament didn't just involve the rich, important bishops and barons. There were also two knights from each county and two from each large town. These people became known as **commoners**, and later the **Commons**. For the first time, ordinary people had some say in how England was run. The Lords and the Commons helped the king run the country and they met in separate buildings or **Houses**. The British Parliament, made up of the House of Lords and the House of Commons, still meets like this today.

De Montfort in distress!

Simon de Montfort was to pay a heavy price for his Parliament. Edward escaped from capture and defeated de Montfort's army at Evesham in August 1265. Simon's body was hacked to pieces and his testicles were cut off and hung around his nose!

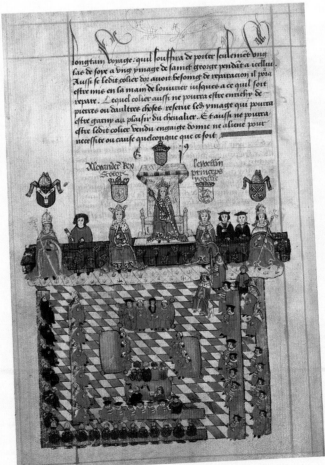

WISE-UP Words

advisors
commoners   Commons
Houses   Parliament

Work

1 a Which mistakes did Henry III make that his father King John also made? Which of these mistakes do you think upset the barons the most? Put them in order of importance.

b Explain what happened in the following years:
- 1216
- 1258
- 1264
- 1265

c What do you think was the most important thing about de Montfort's Parliament? Give reasons for your answer.

The power of Parliament

When Henry III died in 1272, Prince Edward became King Edward I. He didn't want to risk more fights with the barons by scrapping Parliament. Also, if Edward wanted money (which he certainly did) he knew he needed Parliament to get it for him. In return, Parliament would ask the king for permission to introduce new laws. Although it couldn't tell the king what to do, it could certainly make things difficult for him. Power was now firmly with Parliament!

↵ **SOURCE A:** *A medieval document showing a diagram of King Edward I's Parliament.*

_____ **MISSION ACCOMPLISHED?** _____

- Can you explain which mistakes Henry III made that his father also made?
- Do you know what Simon de Montfort did about it?
- Can you explain what important changes de Montfort made to the country that we still have today?

We have seen how the Church and the barons struggled for power with the king. In 1381, it was the turn of the ordinary people in what became known as the Peasants' Revolt. Peasants had very few rights in medieval England, and an argument with their lord would probably end in their death, let alone an argument with the king! So what made the peasants risk their lives and march to London? Who led the peasants on their way? And how worried was the king?

5: The Crown versus the State: The Peasants' Revolt – the build-up

MISSION OBJECTIVES
- To understand why the poorest people in England argued with the king.
- To be aware of the early events of the Peasants' Revolt.

Why were the peasants so fed up?

Before the Black Death, there were lots of workers about. If I didn't work for low wages, there was always someone who would. Now there are far fewer peasants and the lords have to pay me what I ask for. If they don't, there is no one who will do the work! But this new law says I can't earn more money than before the Black Death, and if I ask for more money I will be arrested!

I'm not scared of hard work, but I don't know why I should work for free! I have to work on my lord's land for a couple of days a week and I get nothing for it. This **Work Service** is the law and the lord records all of the hours that I do. If I don't work, I will be arrested!

Never mind the low wages and the Work Service, my problem is the poll tax! The king needs money to pay for his war with France and this year he wants 5 pennies off everybody – rich or poor. Last year it was 1 penny and I struggled to pay that.

... I'M A PEASANT – AND I'M FED UP WITH THE KING! ...

Revolting peasants!

Things turned nasty in May 1381 when King Richard II's officials arrived in the village of Fobbing in Essex to collect the **poll tax**. Three of the king's tax collectors were killed by the peasants but one escaped and rode back to London to tell the king. Word soon spread and other collectors were attacked all over Essex and Kent – the Peasants' Revolt had begun!

Follow the leader!

Thousands of peasants met up in Maidstone, Kent, and chose Wat Tyler, a former soldier, as their leader. He freed a priest called John Ball who had been thrown in Maidstone Jail by the Archbishop of Canterbury. Ball had been travelling around Kent telling people that God had made everybody equal and that they should refuse to do Work Service.

London calling!

By June 1381, there were about 60 000 angry peasants, armed with scythes and pitchforks. They wanted to get to London, talk to the king and change the law. On the way there, the peasant army ran riot. Jails were opened and criminals set free whilst the houses of the rich were set on fire. Manor houses were targeted by the peasants and they often contained important documents like the records of Work Service.

Capital gains!

The city gates were opened by the peasants of London and the capital was flooded with people. The peasants broke into the Savoy Palace, home of the king's hated uncle and advisor, John of Gaunt. It was blown up with gunpowder and all of Gaunt's valuables were thrown into the river. Wat Tyler, worried about **discipline**, beheaded a man for stealing silver and announced that there should be no **looting**. Peasants continued to arrive from all over the country and historians estimate there may have been 100 000 of them.

The king watched from the safety of the Tower of London as his capital city descended into chaos. He sent a message to Tyler and Ball. He would meet them in the area of Mile End the very next day.

⭐ **WISE-UP** Words

discipline
looting
poll tax
revolt
Work Service

Work ⌇

1 Explain how each of the following made the peasants so angry in 1381.

   a The Black Death.

   b Work Service.

   c Poll tax.

2 Match up the names on the left with the correct descriptions on the right.

Wat Tyler	King of England
John Ball	The king's uncle and adviser
Richard II	Leader of the Peasants' Revolt
John of Gaunt	Priest who believed all men were equal and should not be forced to work for free

Wat Tyler had a few options when he met with the king at Mile End. Find an advantage and a disadvantage for each option.

• Burn London to the ground.

• Tell King Richard what you would like to happen and hope he agrees.

• Tell King Richard to agree to your demands or face death.

Which option would you choose? Give reasons for your answer.

___ **MISSION ACCOMPLISHED?** ___

• Could you tell someone three reasons why the peasants became so angry?

• Can you describe and explain how the peasants behaved on the way to London?

On 14 June 1381 King Richard II climbed into a boat and travelled along the Thames to meet the leaders of the peasants at Mile End. Huge angry crowds shouted abuse at him from the river banks. It was the most important and dangerous trip of Richard's life. And he was just 14 years old!

6: The Crown versus the people: The Peasants' Revolt – power to the people?

MISSION OBJECTIVES

- To understand how the Peasants' Revolt ended.
- To be aware of the consequences of the Peasants' Revolt.
- To examine sources of evidence and identify differences and similarities.

Mile End

The leaders of the peasants greeted their king by kneeling down and bowing to him. One of the peasants said, 'We will not have any other king than you.' Wat Tyler explained that the peasants had no problem with the king, but they wanted to work for the highest wages they could get. Also, they didn't want to have to work for free, and they certainly didn't want to pay the new, increased poll tax. To everyone's astonishment, the king agreed to everything! He even said he would give free **pardons** to the peasants who had committed crimes during the revolt. There was just one condition – everyone had to go home! The peasants had won! The people with the least power and money in England had challenged the king and won! Or had they?

Trouble at the tower!

At around the same time that the king was at Mile End, another group of peasants did something that no one had done before or since – they captured the Tower of London! The angry mob dragged away the Archbishop of Canterbury and the man who looked after the king's money – the **Treasurer**. Both men were beheaded and their heads were stuck on spikes and paraded through the streets. The Archbishop's hat – the **mitre** – was nailed to his skull so that everyone would know whose head it was.

❚❚ PAUSE for Thought

It must have taken great courage to go and meet thousands of angry peasants. Why do you think young Richard felt he had to go?

15 June 1381

Richard knew he would have to meet the rebel leaders once more. The Lord Mayor of London came up with the idea of meeting the mob at Smithfield, which was outside the city walls. Medieval London was mostly made of wood and the streets were narrow and cramped. The mayor was worried that if things turned nasty, the peasants would disappear down the winding streets and London would go up in smoke! At Smithfield, the king once again met with Wat Tyler, who was joined by 25 000 peasants. We are not exactly sure what happened next as the only people who could write about it were on the side of the king. Read Sources A and B to see if you can work out what happened.

'At that moment the Mayor of London arrived with 12 knights, all well armed, and broke through to speak to the crowd. He said to Tyler, 'Halt! Would you dare to speak like that in front of the king?' The king began to get angry and told the Mayor, 'Set hands on him.' Tyler said to the Mayor, 'What have I said to annoy you?' 'You lying, stinking, crook,' said the Mayor. 'Would you speak like that in front of the king? By my life, you'll pay dearly for it.' And the Mayor drew his sword and struck Tyler such a blow to the head that he fell down at the feet of his horse. The knights clustered around him so that he couldn't be seen by the rebels. Then a squire called John Standish drew out his sword and put it to Tyler's belly and so he died. Seeing their leader killed, the people began to murmur and said, 'Let us go and kill them all.' And they got themselves ready for battle.'

↳ **SOURCE A:** *This was written by John Froissant, a French knight, who wasn't at the revolt.*

'The commons were arrayed in battle formation in great numbers. Tyler dismounted, carrying his dagger. He called for some water and rinsed his mouth in a very rude disgusting fashion in front of the king. Tyler then made to strike the king's valet [bodyguard] with his dagger. The Mayor of London tried to arrest him, and because of this Wat stabbed the mayor with his dagger in the stomach. But the Mayor, as it pleased God, was wearing armour, and drew his cutlass and gave Wat a deep cut on the neck, and then a great cut on the head.'

↳ **SOURCE B:** *A different account of the meeting at Smithfield.*

WISE-UP Words

individually
mitre pardons
Treasurer

The aftermath!

Whatever actually happened at Smithfield, there was no fighting between the king's men and the peasants. Most set out on the long walk home. King Richard didn't keep any of the promises he had made and his men hunted down the Revolt's ringleaders. John Ball was cut into four pieces in front of the king! The poll tax was scrapped but it looked as if the revolt had been a failure.

However, over the next 50 years, the peasants did receive most of the things they had asked for during the revolt – but on the king's terms! He eventually stopped trying to control the peasants' wages and they were allowed to work for the best wages they could get. Also, the shortage of men to work in the fields meant that they soon became free from their lords. Most importantly, it showed that the peasants, who had no power **individually**, could threaten the king if they joined together.

Work

1 Read Sources A and B. Find two ways in which the two sources are different. Find two ways in which the two sources back each other up.

Why do you think that no peasants wrote down what happened on the 15 June 1381?

Design a newspaper front page for the 16 June 1381 that describes the events of the previous day. Your newspaper supports the king, so make sure your writing is one-sided. Think of a good headline, use quotes and include a picture of the scene.

____ **MISSION ACCOMPLISHED?** ____

- Could you tell someone how the revolt ended for Wat Tyler, John Ball and the king?
- Do you know exactly what happened on the 15 June 1381? Does anyone?

How deadly was the Black Death?

―――――――――――――――― MISSION OBJECTIVES ――――――――――――――――
- Understand the symptoms and spread of the Black Death, the fear it caused and the wide variety of the explanations for its cause.

Look at the painting on this page. Study it carefully. It is a brilliantly detailed and frightening picture about a mysterious killer plague called the Black Death which swept across the world in the Middle Ages. It would kill about 75 million people in Europe!

In the painting, the disease is represented by little killer skeletons who attack people. If you look carefully, you can see them killing all sorts of different people – men, women and children, even a king! And there seems to be no defence against the fearsome killer. It is little wonder that the painting was called 'The Triumph of Death'.

↰ SOURCE A: *'The Triumph of Death'*.

So what exactly was Black Death? How could you catch it? What were the symptoms? What did people at the time think caused it? How did people try to cure it? And what impact did it have on England?

How did it kill people?

The Black Death was a plague. A plague is a disease which spreads quickly. In fact, to be more accurate, the Black Death was two different plagues – **bubonic** plague and **pneumonic** plague – which attacked at the same time. This made the Black Death even deadlier and, before you ask, both plagues still exist today!

These two killer plagues both combined to make the Black Death. It was possible, however, to get one of the plagues without the other. Pneumonic was the deadliest, killing everyone it infected, but 30 per cent of people who caught just bubonic plague survived. Sadly, for millions all over the world, they got both at the same time and stood no chance!

⭐ **WISE-UP** Words

bubonic
pneumonic
flagellant

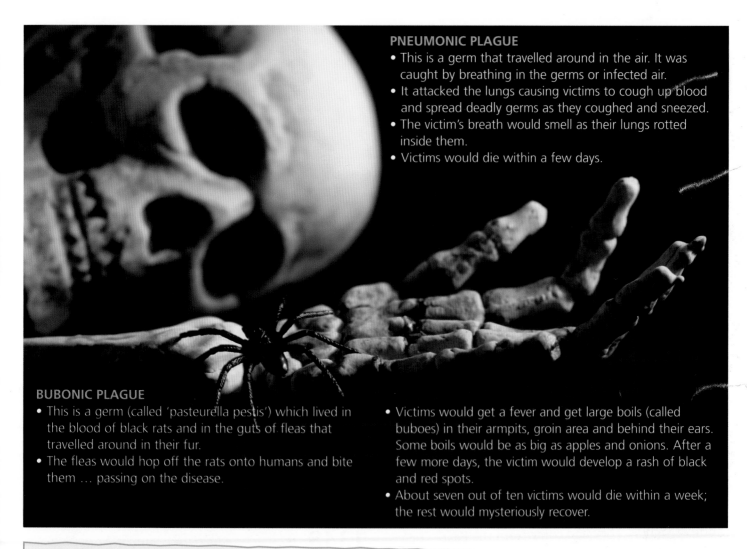

PNEUMONIC PLAGUE
- This is a germ that travelled around in the air. It was caught by breathing in the germs or infected air.
- It attacked the lungs causing victims to cough up blood and spread deadly germs as they coughed and sneezed.
- The victim's breath would smell as their lungs rotted inside them.
- Victims would die within a few days.

BUBONIC PLAGUE
- This is a germ (called 'pasteurella pestis') which lived in the blood of black rats and in the guts of fleas that travelled around in their fur.
- The fleas would hop off the rats onto humans and bite them … passing on the disease.

- Victims would get a fever and get large boils (called buboes) in their armpits, groin area and behind their ears. Some boils would be as big as apples and onions. After a few more days, the victim would develop a rash of black and red spots.
- About seven out of ten victims would die within a week; the rest would mysteriously recover.

i. Lumps in the armpits and the groin. From this, one died in five days.
ii. Fever and spitting of blood. Breathing suffers and whoever has been corrupted cannot live beyond two or three days.
iii. Tumours in the armpits and groin grow as large as apples. Black spots also appear on the arms and thighs.

↵ SOURCE B: *Medieval descriptions of the Black Death.*

Where did it come from?

The Black Death arrived in England at the port of Melcombe Regis in Dorset in 1348. A boatload of sailors brought it with them. It had travelled along trade routes from China and India, through the Middle East, then into Europe through Italy. From there, ships carrying the Plague infected people, and infected rats landed at ports all over Europe.

SOURCE C: *The spread of the Black Death in Europe. The purple areas on the map are the places affected by the plague.*

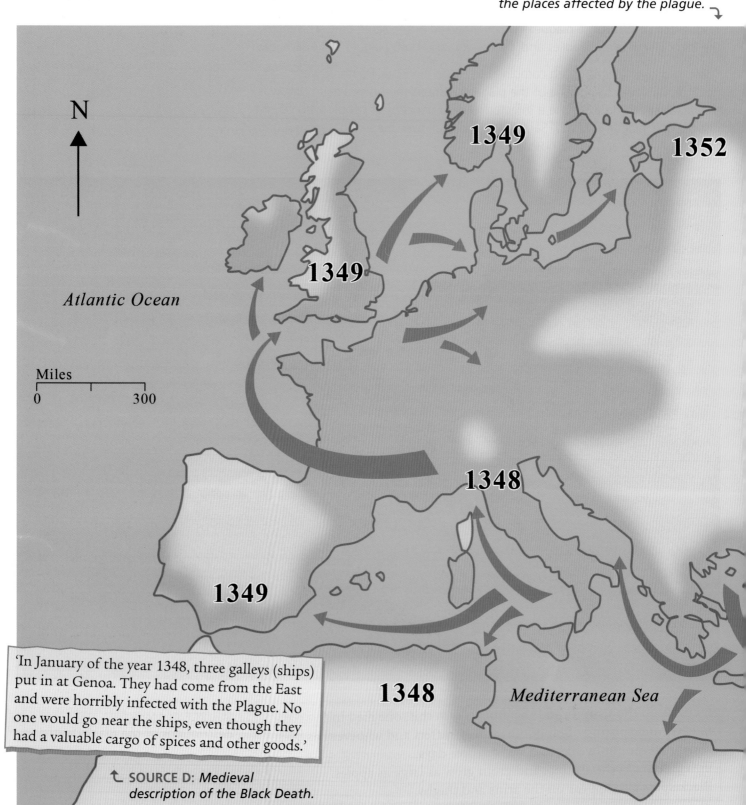

N

Atlantic Ocean

Miles
0   300

1349

1349

1349

1352

1348

1349

1348

Mediterranean Sea

'In January of the year 1348, three galleys (ships) put in at Genoa. They had come from the East and were horribly infected with the Plague. No one would go near the ships, even though they had a valuable cargo of spices and other goods.'

SOURCE D: *Medieval description of the Black Death.*

'In this year at Melcombe (near Weymouth, Dorset), a little before the feast of St John the Baptist (24 June), two ships came into the harbour. One of the sailors had brought him, from Gascony in France, the disease, and through him the people of Melcombe were the first in England to be infected.'

↳ SOURCE E: *From the 'Grey Friars Chronicle', written by monks in 1348.*

'They died by the hundreds, both day and night, and all were thrown in ... ditches and covered with earth. And as soon as those ditches were filled, more were dug. And I, Agnolo di Tura ... buried my five children with my own hands ... And so many died that all believed it was the end of the world.'

↳ SOURCE F: *The Plague in Siena: an Italian Chronicle by Agnolo di Tura.*

'Then the grievous plague came to the sea coasts from Southampton, and came to Bristol, and it was as if all the strength of the town had died, as if they had been hit with sudden death, for there were few who stayed in their beds more than three days, or two days, or even one half a day.'

↳ SOURCE G: *Henry Knighton, an Augustinian Canon at the Abbey of St Mary, Leicester.*

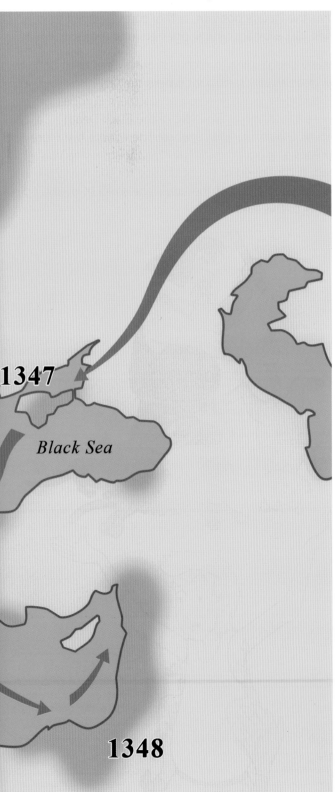

1347

Black Sea

1348

'That disease entirely stripped villages, cities, castles and towns of inhabitants of men, so that scarcely anyone would be able to live in them. The plague was so contagious that those touching the dead or even the sick were immediately infected and died, and the one confessing and the confessor were together led to the grave ... many died from carbuncles and from ulcers and pustules that could be seen on shins and under the armpits; some died, as if in a frenzy, from pain of the head, others from spitting blood ... These cities of Dublin and Drogheda were almost destroyed and wasted of inhabitants and men so that in Dublin alone, from the beginning of August right up to Christmas, fourteen thousand men died ...There was scarcely a house in which only one died but commonly man and wife with their children and family going one way, namely, crossing to death.'

↳ SOURCE H: *Friar John Clyn describing the effects of the plague after its spread to Ireland in August 1348.*

What did people think caused the Black Death?

Doctors didn't know that germs caused disease so looked for other reasons to explain why something so terrible was happening. Sources F to J show the different ways in which people at the time tried to explain the cause of the Plague.

'The plague carried by these cursed Italian ships was a punishment sent by God.'

↰ SOURCE F: *By an Italian writer in the Middle Ages.*

'In many German cities, Jews were thought to have caused the deaths by poisoning the water supply. Many Jewish men, women and children were burned to death for this.'

↰ SOURCE G: *From a book written in 1349.*

'You should avoid overeating and avoid having a bath. These open up the pores of the skin through which the poisonous air can enter.'

↰ SOURCE H: *A French writer, 1365.*

'The long term cause is the position of the planets. It is also caused by evil smells which mix with the air and spread on the wind. When you breathe in the corrupted air you catch the plague.'

↰ SOURCE I: *Based on a report written by doctors at Paris University in 1348.*

'The disease was spread by contagion. If a healthy man visited a plague victim, he usually died himself.'

↰ SOURCE J: *Written by Jean de Venette in 1348.*

How did people try to cure the plague?

Doctors didn't know what caused the Plague so were unable to find a way of curing it and stopping it spread. Some recommended herbal potions to fight the disease, others suggested begging God for help or eating (yes, eating) prayers that had been written down for you. And as the Plague got worse, the 'cures' seemed to get crazier. Just look at those suggested in Source K below.

So many people died that church graveyards filled up. Soon people were left to rot where they fell. However, by 1353, after spreading up into northern Europe (Denmark, Sweden and Norway), the Black Death eventually died out… for a while. There were five more outbreaks of plague before 1400, although none was as bad. It continued to haunt Europe for the next 250 years. As people said at the time, 'the smell of death hangs over this land.'

Why not kill all the cats and dogs?

I've been told that shaving a chicken's bottom and strapping it to the boils will do the trick.

SOURCE K: *Some of the cures suggested at the time. It's easy to laugh at some of them, but try to appreciate that people were scared – not stupid – and were prepared to try anything.* ↱

⬑ SOURCE L: *Some people believed that the Plague was a punishment sent from God for their sins. They thought that the best way to get rid of your wickedness was to beat it out of you. In Europe, large groups of people called* **flagellants** *went around whipping themselves, hoping that God would take pity on them and stop the Plague!*

SOURCE M: *These words were scratched on a church wall in Ashwell, Hertfordshire. They read: '1349 the pestilence. 1350, pitless, wild, violent, the dregs of the people live to tell the tale.'* ↱

↳ **SOURCE N:** *A photograph of a flea carrying the plague. Scientists know it has the plague because of the dark line on the right-hand side of its blood-filled stomach!*

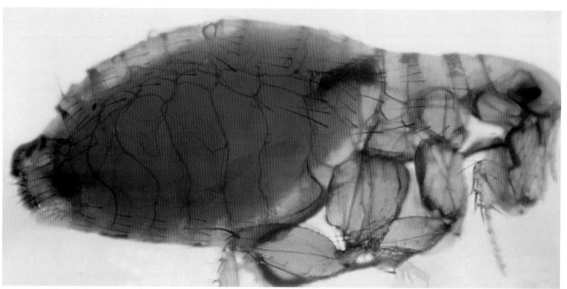

↰ **SOURCE O:** *An illustration from a manuscript showing victims covered in buboes. What might the figure in the background be doing?*

The impact of the Plague

The Black Death had killed about a third of the people in England. The population was about four million before the Plague came – afterwards, there were probably only about two and a half million people left.

This dramatic drop in population meant that life couldn't go on in the same way. There were fewer people to plough the fields and harvest the crops for a start, so tons of wheat, oats and barley just rotted in the fields!

But for the peasants who survived the Plague, the future looked better than ever. The local lords still needed men to work on their land – but there were fewer men. As a result, the workers could ask for higher wages… and they usually got them! Sources P to T look at the effects of the Black Death.

↰ **SOURCE Q:** *This map shows the number of deserted medieval villages after the Plague had killed their inhabitants.*

'The King sent an order to all the counties that labourers should not be paid more than before the plague. But the labourers were so proud and stubborn that they would not listen to the king's command. If anyone wanted to employ then he had to pay them what they wanted or lose his fruit and crops. Then the king ordered many labourers to be arrested and put in prison.'

↰ **SOURCE R:** *From 'Knighton's Chronicle 1337–1396' by Henry Knighton*

'It is sad but the whole world was changed for the worse. People were meaner and more greedy than before, even though they had more things. They were jealous of each other and there was an increase in the number of fights, arguments and law cases.'

↰ **SOURCE S:** *Jean de Venette, 1349.*

'As soon as masters accuse their workers of bad work or try to pay them less they leave and quickly find jobs in new places at higher wages. Masters dare not upset their workers and have to give them whatever they ask for.'

↰ **SOURCE T:** *Introduction to a law, 1376.*

"Sheep and oxen wandered free through the fields and among the crops, and there was nobody to drive them off. When harvest time came, higher wages were not enough to get people to gather in the crops which rotted in the fields."

↰ **SOURCE P:** *From 'Knighton's Chronicle 1337–1396' by Henry Knighton.*

Work

1 Copy and complete the following table:

	Bubonic plague	Pneumonic plague
How was it caught?		
What were the symptoms?		
How long did it take to die?		

Why do you think it was called the 'Black Death'?

2 Look at Source A. What do you think the artist is saying about the Black Death?

3 Look at Sources C, D and E. How did the Black Death spread across Europe?

4 Look at Sources F to J.

   a Make a list of all the different causes of plague you can find in these sources.

   b Why do you think there were so many different explanations of the causes of the Black Death?

   c Which explanation came closest to the real cause the of Black Death?

5 Look at Source L. Why do you think the flagellants behaved as they did?

── **MISSION ACCOMPLISHED?** ──

• Do you know the difference between bubonic and pneumonic plague?

• Can you identify three things that people in 1348 thought caused the Black Death?

Who healed the sick in the Middle Ages?

- To aim to know the theories behind different treatments in the Middle Ages.
- To identify at least two ways that doctors might diagnose an illness.

It is 1350 and you feel ill. If you are poor you might ask people in your village if they know of any treatments. You will probably get a variety of answers telling you to try all sorts of strange herbs, plants and poisons. Some might even make you feel a bit better. But if your neighbours don't help, you might try praying a bit harder or plan a pilgrimage to a holy place and hope that God might cure you. As a last resort, you might take what money you have and travel to the nearest town and see the doctor.

However, he will have no modern drugs like antibiotics or antiseptic (such as Dettol or TCP) to prevent infection. He doesn't know that germ and viruses make us ill either. In fact, he doesn't know much about the real cause of illness at all. So what will he do to make you feel better?

Diagnosis

To find out what was wrong with you, the doctor would probably ask you to wee in a clear glass bottle. He would then examine it three times – once when it's fresh, again when it has been cooling for about an hour and finally when it has gone completely cold. He might even taste it to see if it was sweet or sour, bitter or salty. He would probably examine your blood too, look at your tongue and take your pulse. He might even ask you to poo on a tray so he could have a good look through it!

Your doctor would then go off to look at his charts and flick through his books. The colour of your urine would be matched against the shades on a special diagram – they did this because they thought that every shade had a different meaning.

! FACT Dodgy cures

Good doctors were in short supply and could be expensive. This left things open for quacks, people who sell all sorts of potions that are supposed to cure everything. These potions were sold at fairs and by the side of roads... and usually contained nothing at all to help you to get better!

A bloody mess

Your doctor might also believe that your own blood was a cause of illness. This was based on an old Greek idea that too much blood in a person's body could make them ill. Many doctors thought that the answer was to make the patient bleed, so that their 'bad' blood would disappear and their body would be in balance again. This was called **blood-letting** and special tools and bowls were used to cut open a vein and bleed a patient. Sometimes **leeches** were used to suck the blood out too. If you were selected for a bleeding session you would pray your doctor was skilled enough to know when to stop before you lost too much blood!

WISE-UP Words

barber-surgeon
blood-letting
leeches
trepanning

'If you would strength and fitness keep,
shun care and anger while you sleep.
All heavy food and wine give up,
and noon day slumber too must stop.
Walk awhile each day you should,
for this will only do you good.
These rules obey and you will find,
long life is yours and peaceful mind.'

↳ **SOURCE A:** *A medieval poem which proves that there were some very sensible ideas about health and fitness long ago.*

'A doctor must know how to read so that he can understand medical books. He must know how to write and speak well so that he can explain the diseases he is treating. He must have a good mind to investigate and cure the causes of disease. Arithmetic is also important, so that he can be a great help to the sick. Lastly, he must know astronomy so that he can study the stars and the seasons, because our bodies change with the planets and stars.'

↳ **SOURCE B:** *An early medieval writer (Isidore, c.620).*

"
Doctors possess three special qualifications and these are: to be able to lie without being caught out; to pretend to be honest; and to cause death without feeling guilty.
"

↳ **SOURCE C:** *Written in 1380.*

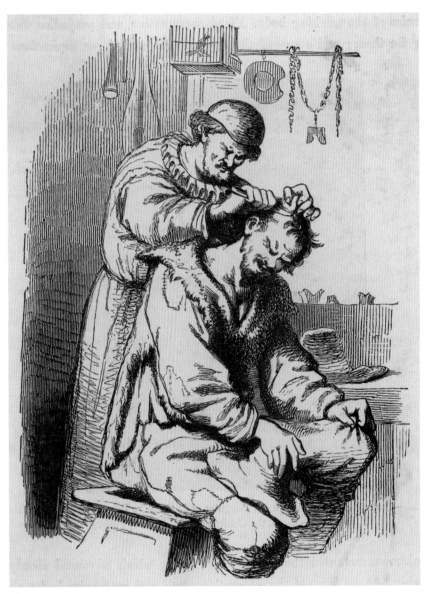

↳ **SOURCE D:** *If your doctor recommended a blood-letting session, you might get the job done by a **barber-surgeon**. He was usually a bit cheaper than a doctor and you could have your hair cut at the same time (sharp knives you see!). His shop would be easy to spot because it had a red and white pole outside (red for blood, white for bandages). Some barbers still have poles like these outside their shops today.*

Treatment

Many doctors treated patients by blood-letting or purging (see Source E), but they would also know lots of other ways to try to make you better. For a start, your doctor would have access to all sorts of strange mixtures and potions and would often delve into their notes for any old traditional recipes or treatments. But whether you got well or not was very hit and miss. Source F shows a number of strange cures used by doctors in the Middle Ages that appeared in a book published at the time.

SOURCE E: *Some doctors preferred purging to blood-letting in order to get your body back in balance. He would usually give you something to make you vomit or even give you an enema (a mixture of water, bran, salt, honey and soap) that was squirted up your bottom through a greasy pipe!* ↱

For an ache that is found in the teeth, take a whole corn of pepper and chew on them.

For swollen eyes, take a live crab, poke out its eyes and put it back in the water. Stick the eyes onto your neck and you will be well.

For wheezing and shortness of breath, kill a fox and take out its liver and lungs. Chop them up and mix it with wine. Then drink the mixture out of a church bell.

If you are bitten by a snake, smear ear wax on the bite, then ask the priest to say a prayer for you.

If you accidentally drink an insect in the water, find a sheep, cut into it and drink the blood while it's still hot. If you take good long gulps, all will be well.

For warts, hold a live toad next to the skin and soon your skin will soften and the warts will disappear.

↰ **SOURCE F:** *Medieval treatments!*

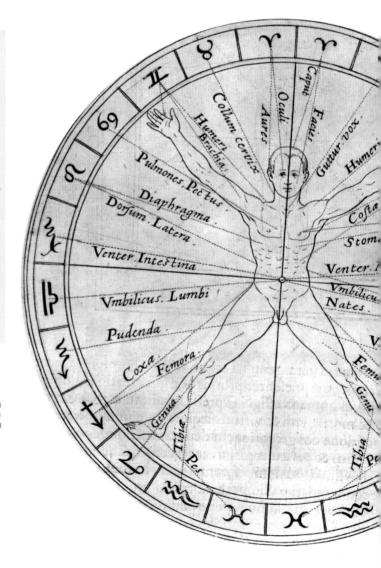

✚ **Hungry for MORE**
In pairs write a short script for a role-play activity about a sick person's visit to the doctor in the Middle Ages. One person should act out the role of patient, the other the role of the doctor. Look back at this section for some gruesome ideas!

↵ **SOURCE G:** *A common 'cure' for a headache in the Middle Ages was to ask a doctor to drill a hole in the side of your head. People believed this would let out the evil spirits trapped there. This method was called **trepanning**.*

Plants and herbs – like clover, poppy, willow leaves and garlic – were used a lot in the Middle Ages too. Today we know that their use must have had real success. Modern scientists recently analysed a medieval medicine book and concluded that over half of the herbal remedies prescribed to ease pain and help fight infection would have actually worked. Poppies and willow leaves, for example, contain a natural form of painkiller, whilst garlic is known to kill bacteria.

Poppy

Willow leaves

Garlic

Work

1 Make a list of the treatments used by doctors to cure people in the Middle Ages. For each treatment see if you can explain why a doctor might have believed the treatment would work.

2 Read Source C.

  a What is this person's opinion of doctors in 1380?

  b Can you think of any reasons why the person might have thought this?

3 Read Source I.

  a Who appears to have the best understanding of medicine – the European doctor or the Arabic doctor? Explain your answer.

  b European doctors' understanding of medicine improved greatly after many years of war against the Arabs. Why do you think this might have happened?

4 Study Source G.

  a Explain in detail what is happening in the picture.

  b Does this source in any way back up the views in Source C? Explain your answer.

SOURCE H: *A zodiac chart. If doctors needed to operate, they would use a zodiac chart to find a safe date. The chart showed a man surrounded by figures to show which constellations (groups of stars) were thought to 'rule' different parts of the body. Different parts had to be left alone during the time when its stars were high in the sky!*
↵

'An Arab doctor was asked to treat a knight with a cut on his leg and a woman with lung disease. He cleaned the knight's leg and put a fresh dressing on it and changed the woman's diet to make her feel better.

A European doctor appeared and laughed at the Arab doctor's ideas. He told the knight that it would be better for him to live with one leg than not to live at all and ordered that the wounded leg should be removed. The knight died with one swing of the axe.

The European doctor then cut open the woman's skull and removed her brain. He rubbed the brain with salt, claiming that this would wash away the devil inside her. The woman, of course, died instantly.'

⤷ **SOURCE I:** *European and Arabic treatments.*

! FACT
Surgeons were often viewed as being no better than butchers. They didn't need to go to university but did need to pass a test to get their licence. They pulled teeth, lanced boils, treated burns, set broken bones and let blood. Military surgeons were experts at removing arrowheads and repairing cuts.

—MISSION ACCOMPLISHED?—

• Can you recall at least two ways doctors might diagnose illness in the Middle Ages, and explain what treatment they might give you?

How healthy were England's kings?

• To develop an opinion – do you think England's kings were a particularly healthy bunch?

Would you like to have been a king of England during the Middle Ages? Surely it was one of the best jobs in the world – a luxury lifestyle with all the best clothes, the finest homes and the tastiest food. You would have all the brightest, best and most hard-working people in the land to attend to your every need. But could a king's great status, wealth and power buy them a long and happy life? Indeed, just how healthy were England's kings?

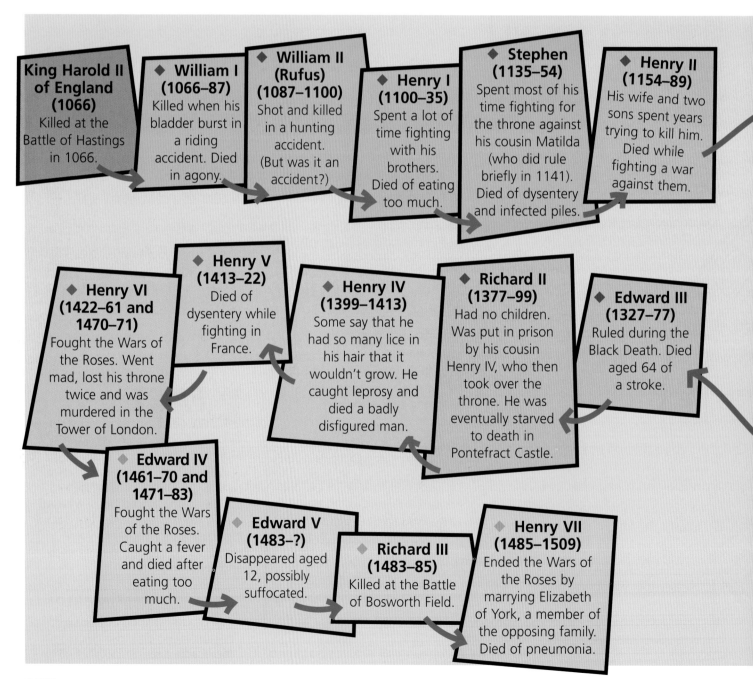

King Harold II of England (1066)
Killed at the Battle of Hastings in 1066.

William I (1066–87)
Killed when his bladder burst in a riding accident. Died in agony.

William II (Rufus) (1087–1100)
Shot and killed in a hunting accident. (But was it an accident?)

Henry I (1100–35)
Spent a lot of time fighting with his brothers. Died of eating too much.

Stephen (1135–54)
Spent most of his time fighting for the throne against his cousin Matilda (who did rule briefly in 1141). Died of dysentery and infected piles.

Henry II (1154–89)
His wife and two sons spent years trying to kill him. Died while fighting a war against them.

Henry VI (1422–61 and 1470–71)
Fought the Wars of the Roses. Went mad, lost his throne twice and was murdered in the Tower of London.

Henry V (1413–22)
Died of dysentery while fighting in France.

Henry IV (1399–1413)
Some say that he had so many lice in his hair that it wouldn't grow. He caught leprosy and died a badly disfigured man.

Richard II (1377–99)
Had no children. Was put in prison by his cousin Henry IV, who then took over the throne. He was eventually starved to death in Pontefract Castle.

Edward III (1327–77)
Ruled during the Black Death. Died aged 64 of a stroke.

Edward IV (1461–70 and 1471–83)
Fought the Wars of the Roses. Caught a fever and died after eating too much.

Edward V (1483–?)
Disappeared aged 12, possibly suffocated.

Richard III (1483–85)
Killed at the Battle of Bosworth Field.

Henry VII (1485–1509)
Ended the Wars of the Roses by marrying Elizabeth of York, a member of the opposing family. Died of pneumonia.

! FACT The name game

Historians give names to the different groups or families who ruled England between 1066 and 1485. This also makes it easier to remember the stories about them.

KEY

◆ Norman, because they first lived in Normandy, France

◆ Plantagenet – family name

◆ Lancaster – family name

◆ York – family name

◆ Tudor – family name

Work

1 Make notes of how many kings were killed by the following:
   - battle accident • eating too much
   - murder • old age • illness

2 Draw a bar chart to show your findings.

3 What was the biggest cause of death? Why do you think this was so high?

4 Which cause of death surprises you the most? Explain your answer.

5 Write a paragraph to answer the following question: 'Was being a medieval King of England a dangerous job?'

◆ **Richard I (The Lionheart) (1189–99)**

Shot in the neck by an arrow while fighting in France. The wound became infected when doctors tried to dig out the arrow tip. Died as a result of the infection.

◆ **John (Lackland) (1199–1216)**

Spent a lot of his time arguing with his barons. Died from dysentery, made worse by eating too many peaches.

◆ **Henry III (1216–72)**

Thrown into prison by Simon de Montfort in 1264. Eventually regained his throne in 1265 but had lost the respect of his barons. Died of old age.

◆ **Edward II (1307–27)**

Lost all the land in Scotland that his father had won. Hated by his wife Isabella, who wanted their son to be king instead. She eventually killed him by ordering two men to stick a red-hot iron up his bottom!

◆ **Edward I (Hammer of the Scots) (1272–1307)**

Died of dysentery while on his way to fight the Scots.

Success

MISSION ACCOMPLISHED?

- Can you remember how five of England's kings met their death?

129

The topic of crime and punishment is big news. The latest crime figures, the big murder trials and the state of our prisons are issues that are always on our television screens, on the radio and in the newspapers and magazines. As a result, today we are quite well informed about law and order. We know that, generally speaking, the police investigate crime and catch as many law-breakers as they can. We also know that the courts decide on a person's guilt, and any guilty person is punished by a fine or even prison. But what was it like in the Middle Ages? How were criminals caught? What were their trials like? Were these trials fair? And how were people punished?

1: Keeping the peace

MISSION OBJECTIVES
• To understand, and be able to explain, how criminals were caught, tried and punished in the Middle Ages.

Keeping the peace

There were no policemen in the Middle Ages. If towns and villages wanted to keep law and order they had to do it themselves. If you ever saw someone committing a crime you had to raise the **hue and cry**. This meant that you had to shout loudly and people would come to help you track down or catch the criminal.

In some areas, all men and women over the age of 12 were grouped into ten. These **tithings**, as they were known, were responsible for each other's behaviour. If a member of the tithing broke the law the others had to take him or her to court and pay their fines.

Some places set up a **watch** – a group of people who patrolled the streets each night – and a **constable** was chosen to coordinate them. But these weren't particularly popular jobs. People didn't get paid for a start… and you lost a lot of sleep whilst walking around the streets all night. As a result, constables and watchmen didn't always do their jobs properly – if they did, they might be chosen again.

Because there was no police force, criminals must have got away with very serious crimes because they were never caught. So sometimes even the king himself got involved in investigations. In 1129, for example, King Henry I fined four whole villages for not finding a murderer quickly enough.

'The township of Stansfield did not raise the hue and cry on the thieves that burgled the house of Amery of Hertelay, nor ever found or prosecuted them. They are to be fined 40 shillings.'

⤶ **SOURCE A:** *From Halifax Manor court records, 18 October 1315.*

On trial

When caught for a minor crime, the criminal would usually be taken to the local lord's manor house. The lord would then decide on the punishment, which would usually be a fine. This was a good way for the lord to raise money. Sometimes, though, the guilty person was humiliated by what was called a 'showing punishment' like being tied up and whipped. This took place in the centre of the village as a warning to others. Source B shows genuine crimes and their punishments from Manor Courts in the 1300s.

- Nicholas Hopwood for hitting Magota, daughter of Henry – fined 2d.
- Margaret Webb for breach of peace – fined 2d.
- Amos Walter for theft of his lord's pigs. Also carrying a bow and arrow in his lord's wood – two fingers on right hand struck off; fined 2d for bow and arrow.

↰ SOURCE B: *Stone Manor Court, November 1335.*

! FACT Escaping punishment

If you were 'on the run', there were several ways to escape punishment. You could hide in a church and claim **sanctuary**. This meant you would be safe in the church for 40 days. If you confessed your crime after 40 days, you were made to leave the country and avoid punishment. However, you would have to carry a large wooden cross to the nearest port! Alternatively, if you could read a verse from the Bible (and not many could), you could claim **benefit of the clergy**. This meant you had the right to go on trial in a **Church Court**, usually reserved for priests. These courts imposed much lighter sentences than any other.

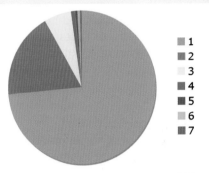

1 Theft (73.5%)
2 Murder (18.2%)
3 Receiving stolen goods (6.2%)
4 Arson (0.8%)
5 Counterfeiting (0.6%)
6 Rape (0.5%)
7 Treason (0.2%)

↰ SOURCE C: *To give you an idea of the types of crime committed in the Middle Ages, this pie chart shows the most common offences prosecuted in eight counties between 1300 and 1348.*

two men caught fighting   a baker being punished for selling stale bread   a drunk in the stocks

More serious crimes were dealt with by county courts. These were sometimes known as Shire courts or Royal courts. A judge appointed by the king, would travel to each county (perhaps twice a year) to deal with any crimes thought too serious for the local lord to deal with. Working with advisors, the judge would work through the evidence, listen to witnesses and come to a verdict. If the case was unclear, the judge may order a **trial by ordeal** as a way of letting God (who everyone believed in) decide on someone's guilt. Trial by ordeal, the judge felt, was a good way for God to help the innocent… and punish the guilty.

The most common ordeals were by fire, by water and by combat:

ORDEAL BY FIRE

Step 1 The accused carries a red-hot iron bar for three steps, or takes a stone from the bottom of a pot of boiling water.

Step 2 The prisoner's hand is bandaged, and he returns to court three days later.

Verdict If the wound has healed, God must think the prisoner is worth helping and so he must be innocent. If the wound is infected, God must think the prisoner is not worth healing and so he must be guilty. He must be punished by being put to death.

ORDEAL BY WATER

Step 1 The accused is tied up.

Step 2 He is thrown into a lake or river.

Verdict Water is pure, just like God. If the prisoner floats, the water doesn't want him, nor does God. If God has rejected him, he must be guilty. He was put to death. If the prisoner sinks and drowns, God must want him in heaven. He must be innocent.

ORDEAL BY COMBAT

This was a trial for rich people. The accuser would fight the accused. It was possible to get someone called a champion to fight for you. For some people this was their job, earning huge amounts of money fighting on behalf of different lords.

Step 1 Both sides should select their weapons. These would be made from wood and bone.

Step 2 The accuser and the accused (or their champions) must fight for as long as possible, starting at sunrise.

Verdict People believed God would give the winner extra strength. The first person to surrender was thought to be guilty and therefore must be punished by being put to death.

Thankfully, trial by ordeal didn't last long. They were stopped early in the thirteenth century, when church leaders objected to them. Instead they were gradually replaced by a system still used today – trial by **jury**. The jury was a group of 12 local men who had the job of saying whether the person was telling the truth or not. The judge then decided if the person was guilty. In later years, the jury would decide on a guilty or innocent verdict – something that still survives in today's crown courts.

Punishment fits the crime

The most common form of punishment, usually for minor crimes was a fine. After, all this was a good way for a local lord or the king to raise money. But the punishments for the more serious crimes could be brutal. Murderers, for example, would be executed – in any number of different ways! The most common form of execution was to hang the offender from a tree but some areas used more vicious methods. In Kent, a murderer might be buried alive, in Portsmouth they would be burned to death and in Pevensey they might be thrown off the bridge into the harbour to drown! And all punishments, including execution, took place in public as a warning to others.

CRIMES AND THEIR PUNISHMENTS

The most serious crimes are at the top, the least serious at the bottom.

**High treason
(a crime against king or country):**

| hanging | drawing | quartering |

Murder, manslaughter, stealing anything worth a lot of money:

| men hanged | women usually burned |

Smaller crimes like fighting, drunkenness or small thefts:

| fines | hand cut off |

| stocks or pillory | whipping |

In fact, public humiliation was thought the best way to 'teach' offenders a lesson – and the best way to discourage others. A drunk or a pair of street fighters, for example, might be sentenced to spend some time in the **stocks** or the **pillory**. And punishments were often thought up to fit the crime. For example, a fishmonger who sold bad fish might have his rotten food tied around his neck whilst he was dragged through the streets on a wooden sledge. Passers-by would be encouraged to throw rotten fruit or shout abuse at him. Thieves might have a few fingers chopped off!

Work

1 Match each word or phrase in List A with the correct definition from list B.

List A	List B
Tithing	A loud noise to make people chase a criminal
Hue and cry	A group of 10 people responsible for each other
Jury	An official who looked after law and order
Stocks	A group who watched over a town
Constable	A wooden frame used to hold prisoners
Watch	A group of men who decided if a prisoner was telling the truth

2 Look at source B.

  a What crimes has Amos Walter committed?

  b Why do you think Amos was punished in this way?

3 a List the three types of ordeal.

  b Why do you think people in the Middle Ages believed that ordeals were the best way to find out if a person was guilty or not?

  c Do you think ordeals were a good way of finding out if someone was guilty? Why do you think that punishments in the Middle Ages were so brutal? Give reasons for your views.

MISSION ACCOMPLISHED?

- Can you explain what is meant by the terms 'hue and cry', 'trial by ordeal' and 'hung, drawn and quartered'?

ENGLAND AT WAR

Conflict or war was a regular feature of the Middle Ages. Sometimes it was barons against each other or the king and sometimes the Royal Family fought each other for the right to rule England. And then there were wars against neighbouring countries. In fact, many people in medieval England believed that a good king was one powerful enough to control the country and who used force to take over other nations. So why did some of these wars take place? Why did English kings want to control their neighbours?

What was Edward I's 'Ring of Iron'?

MISSION OBJECTIVES

- To understand how and why Edward I tried to control Wales.
- To know what was special about the castles of the 'Ring of Iron'.

In the thirteenth century Edward I invaded Wales and built castles that became known as the 'Ring of Iron'. This was England's golden age of castle building, the cost was enormous, more money than Edward could afford. What was so different about the 'Ring of Iron'? And where did Edward get his ideas for this new series of castles?

Wales in the Middle Ages

In the Middle Ages, the Welsh did not have a king but instead each area had its own chief. When William conquered England, he gave the land on the Welsh border to his most trusted barons. These became known as the **lords of the marches** (marches means borders) and they conquered large parts of South Wales – but the mountainous north still belonged to the independent Welsh tribes.

Llywelyn – the Prince of Wales

In 1258 a Welsh tribal leader called Llywelyn II defeated his rivals and started to call himself the Prince of Wales. In 1272 Edward I became King in England, and decided to show just who was the boss! Edward demanded Llywelyn pay **homage** to him – meaning he had to publicly declare Edward was his ruler. Llywelyn refused and young Edward knew this meant one thing – war!

Invasion number one!

In 1277, Edward I invaded Wales. Three separate English armies marched into the mountains while English ships cut off Llywelyn's food supply from the island of Anglesey. The Welsh prince soon asked Edward for peace and, although he lost most of his land, he was allowed to keep his title.

Invasion number two!

In March 1282, Llywelyn and his brother David rose up in rebellion against the English. This time, there was no negotiating with Llywelyn and in battle the Welsh prince was skewered with a lance by an English knight. His brother David was captured and executed; both of their heads were stuck on spikes at the Tower of London. The death of Llywelyn knocked the fight out of the Welsh fighters and by 1284, all of Wales was in Edward's hands. Llywelyn II was the last leader of a free Welsh nation.

Edward decides to stay

Edward was sick of fighting Welsh rebellions. He was determined that no one in Wales would dare argue with English rule again. He made his eldest son, and heir to the throne, the Prince of Wales. This tradition has continued ever since and the first-born son of the English monarch is always made the Prince of Wales. Edward's next trick was to borrow an idea from William the Conqueror, combined with some ideas he learned while on the Crusades.

The English towns inside Wales

Edward had been amazed by the castles he had seen while fighting in the Holy Land, and thought they would work with the rebellious Welsh. He built a ring of 17 castles all around the mountainous area of Snowdonia in North Wales. The main castles – Harlech, Caernarfon, Conwy, Beaumaris and Rhuddlan, all had **bastide** towns attached to them. Protected by the castles, they were little bits of England inside Wales – Welsh people were not allowed to live there. In fact, they weren't even allowed inside the town gates after dark. Edward persuaded English people to move to these bastide towns on the promise of not taxing them. Edward began to dominate Wales through English castles, English towns and Englishmen.

The Master of the King's Works in Wales

The man given the job of designing the 'Ring of Iron' was an Italian called James of Saint George. He borrowed the idea of bastide towns from France and, rather than building **keeps** inside the castles, he made them **concentric**. To allow his castles to survive a seige for as long as possible, he built many of them backing on to the sea. Supplies could therefore always be guaranteed.

Beaumaris

Conwy

Rhuddlan

Carnaevon

Harlech

Work

1 a Explain why Edward decided to invade Wales in 1277.

b Was he right to send his army to Wales? Explain your answer.

c Why do you think Llywelyn II is sometimes called Llywelyn the Last?

2 Complete the sentences by matching the two halves…

James of Saint George built concentric castles…
English people who moved to Wales…
The castles could survive a siege…
Edward's son was made…

…were kept safe in bastide towns.
…the Prince of Wales.
…which were hard to attack because they had no keeps.
…because they backed on to the sea.

WISE-UP Words

bastide
concentric
homage
keeps
lords of the marches

MISSION ACCOMPLISHED?

- Can you explain how Edward kept Wales under control?
- Could you describe one special feature of Edward's castles that made them hard to attack?

After conquering Wales, Edward I looked north to Scotland. Like Wales, Scotland is a mountainous land that was never controlled by either the Romans or the Normans. During the Middle Ages, the Scots in the Highlands lived in tribes or clans, each with a clan chief. There was, however, an overall King of Scotland who often fought with the King of Norway to the north and the King of England to the south. So, what made Edward I interfere with Scotland? Did he manage to gain control of it? And how does this effect how Scottish people view their country today?

2: Did Edward hammer the Scots?

MISSION OBJECTIVES

- To understand why Edward I invaded Scotland.
- To decide whether Edward I deserved the title of 'The Hammer of the Scots'.

Scottish homage

In 1286 the Scottish King, Alexander III, died without a clear heir. Thirteen men all claimed to be the rightful King of Scotland! In order to sort out the mess, the Scots asked the King of England, Edward I, to choose for them. He picked John Balliol, who agreed to pay homage to Edward. But in 1294, England went to war with France and Balliol saw his chance to break free from English control. This was not something that Edward was prepared to accept and it meant only one thing – war! By 1296, Balliol was captured and thrown in jail. Like Wales, Scotland was now in the hands of Edward I… or was it?

Braveheart?

In 1297, a Scottish knight named William Wallace started a rebellion against English rule. He won a famous victory at Stirling Bridge. Edward again marched north to deal with the rebels and Wallace and his men fled to the mountains. In 1305, Wallace was finally caught and taken to London. He was hung, drawn and quartered in front of a large crowd and his head was put on a spike on London Bridge.

! **FACT** **A famous stone**
Scottish kings had long been crowned at the Stone of Scone or Stone of Destiny. In 1296, Edward I stole the stone and took it to London where it was placed underneath his Coronation Throne. Only in 1996 was it returned to Edinburgh Castle. However, every time a new monarch is crowned, the stone will be borrowed and placed under the Coronation throne in London. ↪

'You seized my castles and land without any excuse. You robbed me and my subjects. You took Scotsmen off to England to be prisoners in your castles. Things just go from bad to worse. Now you have crossed the border with a great army and have started killing and burning.'

↰ SOURCE A: *Part of a letter from John Balliol to Edward I in 1296.*

'John Balliol, the King of Scotland, promised to obey me. Then he and some of his nobles began a plot against me. English ships that were in Scottish ports were burned, and the sailors were killed. An army of Scots invaded England. They burned villages, monasteries and churches. In one place, they set fire to a school with the children still in it. I could stand it no more. So I declared war and invaded Scotland.'

↰ SOURCE B: *Part of a letter from Edward I to the Pope in 1301, explaining his actions.*

O Flower of Scotland,
When will we see
Your like again,
That fought and died for,
Your wee bit Hill and Glen,
And stood against him,
Proud Edward's Army,
And sent him homeward,
Tae think again.

The War of Independence

Wallace's rebellion had completely failed but he had aroused **patriotic** feelings in Scotland. In 1306, the Scots united behind a new leader, Robert Bruce, who was both a general and king. Edward went north to face him but died on the journey before he could fight Bruce. He was 68 years old and left clear instructions for what he wanted on his grave: 'Here is Edward I, the Hammer of the Scots.'

The invasion continued under the new king, Edward II, but he was a weak king and a poor leader. Bruce won battles and captured many English castles between 1307 and 1314. Edward forced a final showdown in June 1314 and sent an enormous army of 25 000 to crush Bruce's 7000 soldiers. The two sides met at Bannockburn near Stirling and, despite being massively outnumbered, the Scots crushed the English in a single day. Edward II returned home with what was left of his army. Robert Bruce remained king and Scotland was to remain a completely separate country from England for the next 300 years.

✚ Hungry for MORE

In the 1990s, the Hollywood star Mel Gibson made a film about William Wallace called *Braveheart*. Many historians criticised the film because parts of the story were invented to make it more exciting. Others praised the film as it got people interested in history.

WISE-UP Words

clans
Highlands
patriotic

Work

1 a Read Source A. What can you learn from Source A about how Edward treated Scotland?

 b Now read Source B. What can you learn from Source B about Edward's reasons for invading Scotland?

2 Why do think Edward placed the Stone of Scone under his throne in England?

3 Write a fact file on the following three figures from Scottish History:
 • John Balliol • William Wallace • Robert the Bruce
 You must explain:
 • their role in Scottish history;
 • what happened to them.
 Give them a thistle rating; 5 thistles – a Highland legend, 1 thistle – a Lowland loser. Give reasons for your thistle ratings.

4 Read Source C. Why do think Edward's invasion is mentioned in Scotland's national anthem?

5 Do you think Edward I deserves his title of 'Hammer of the Scots'? Give reasons for your answer.

MISSION ACCOMPLISHED?

• Can you explain why Edward I marched his armies in to Scotland on two separate occasions?

• Do you know why Edward I called himself 'The Hammer of the Scots' and have you decided if he deserved the title?

The next major war that took place in the British Isles didn't involve England fighting another nation. It became known as the War of the Roses and saw Englishmen fighting Englishmen for control of the throne. So who were the contenders for the Crown? Why did they end up fighting? And who came out smelling of roses?

3: Why was there a War of the Roses?

MISSION OBJECTIVES

• To understand why England went to war with itself in the fifteenth century.
• To know who fought in the War of the Roses and which side ended up with the English Crown.

In 1453, England faced a serious problem: King Henry VI was suffering from a bout of madness. He had lost his memory and would sit silently in the corner of a room for hours on end. He was completely unaware that his wife had given birth to his son. For the powerful York family, this latest episode of **insanity** was a step too far. They thought that they had a strong claim to the throne and they were sure that they could do a better job of running the country. And they were prepared to plunge the country into **civil war** to prove it!

'The great families of the Barons died in the turmoil they had started. They perished, however, alone. The Wars of the Roses hardly touched the common people.'

⌕ SOURCE A: *G. Warner and C. Marten, The Groundwork of British History, 1923.*

'The crown of England had changed hands several times over the past 30 years. Now all the Yorkist leaders were dead except Edward, the Earl of Warwick, and he was safely imprisoned in the Tower where he was murdered in 1499. The Wars of the Roses were at an end and the Tudor dynasty finally secure.'

⌕ SOURCE B: *Philip Haigh, The Military Campaigns of the Wars of the Roses, 1995*

NB arrows show the swapping of the throne between each house

House of Lancaster

House of York

Henry VI 1422–61

Edward IV 1461–70

Henry VI 1470–71

Edward IV 1470

but was murdered in 1471

Edward IV 1471–83

Henry Tudor wins Bosworth, and becomes…

…Henry VII and marries Elizabeth of York 1485–1509

Edward V

Richard III 1483–85…

…but lost Battle of Bosworth 1485

Both houses are united and the War of the Roses is over!

Flower power!

Both the House of York and the House of Lancaster had chosen a rose as their family symbol. The Yorks had chosen a white rose while the Lancasters used a red one. Because of this, historians in the eighteenth century started to call the wars that took place in England between 1461 and 1485 the War of the Roses.

SOURCE C:
The Tudor Rose. ↱

↵ **SOURCE D:**
The England rugby shirt.

❗ FACT Rugby's rose

When Henry Tudor united the two Houses and married Elizabeth of York, he also joined their roses. The York and Lancaster roses were combined to produce the red and white **Tudor Rose** (see Source C). This rose can be seen today on the shirts of the England rugby union team (see Source D).

WISE-UP Words

civil war
insanity
Tudor Rose

Work ⌇.

1

X	F	E	J	T	H	H	B	D	T	U	D	O	R	D
L	P	M	S	L	P	O	L	R	R	S	Z	Y	L	E
K	L	R	V	T	S	Z	A	R	Z	A	R	V	I	Y
F	D	O	U	W	Z	N	N	O	S	N	W	W	C	O
E	Y	D	O	U	B	S	C	V	E	W	Q	D	T	R
R	S	R	C	N	D	R	A	H	C	I	R	B	E	K
T	T	O	V	I	P	I	S	E	Q	R	S	M	O	P
H	R	B	Q	Q	I	K	T	A	I	Y	O	Q	I	K
V	X	Z	S	F	D	T	E	E	V	C	S	W	C	D
H	C	M	E	K	G	E	R	N	W	O	K	P	N	T
V	Z	T	S	N	D	W	E	D	O	Q	Y	C	I	W
Z	A	R	O	U	M	B	K	C	E	J	N	Y	J	S
Z	K	U	R	L	A	W	X	T	K	B	K	A	E	B
B	T	K	L	P	E	N	G	A	S	O	K	F	K	U
A	Q	N	S	T	G	O	D	E	Z	K	P	W	B	Z

BOSWORTH
CROWN
EDWARD
HENRY
LANCASTER
RICHARD
ROSES
TUDOR
YORK

MISSION ACCOMPLISHED?

- Do you know why England had a civil war in the fifteenth century?
- Can you name the families that fought each other?
- Could you explain how these wars got their name?
- Do you know who won the War of the Roses?

Medieval warfare was a horrific experience. Unless you were an archer or crossbowman, fighting meant you'd be close enough to the man you were killing to smell the fear on his breath. You would feel your weapon slice through his flesh and crunch through his bones. At any moment, you could lose an arm or a leg or be stabbed straight through and left to die an agonising death on the battlefield. Improvements in technology and changes in fashion saw a variety of weapons used in the Middle Ages. Study these pages – and choose your weapons!

4: Choose your weapons!

MISSION OBJECTIVES

- To be aware of the different weapons that were used in medieval warfare.
- To decide which weapons were the most effective and explain why.

Pike

One of the most basic weapons on the battlefield, it was perfect for footsoldiers facing knights on horseback. Charging knights would be brought to the ground by large groups of pike-wielding men who stabbed the horse beneath them.

Caltrop

These iron spikes were thrown on the ground in order to stab through the feet of charging horses and men.

Swords of honour

At the beginning of the Middle Ages, swords were large chopping weapons with a razor-sharp double-edged blade. As armour became stronger, shorter swords with extremely sharp points became more popular. Falchions were also used to hack and chop arms, legs and heads off. These were short, fat swords with just one sharpened edge.

Is this a dagger I see before me?

Many men chose to take a dagger with them into battle. It was small and light and meant they weren't completely unarmed if they lost their main weapon. It also came in useful when things got up close and personal and was often used to finish opponents off!

Knight clubbing!

In around 1300, the mace made its first appearance. This was a heavy metal club with short, thick blades – or flanges. It was brought crashing down onto opponents, shattering bones and crushing skulls – even if they were protected by chain mail.

The tale of the flail!

Flails appeared in around 1500. Because of the chain they could be swung much faster and with much greater force than a mace. They were often used to stick into armour and drag knights from the back of their horses where a terrible fate awaited them on the ground.

Axe attack!

Battle axes and poll axes were devastating weapons that could slice a man in half with a single blow. A lot of space was needed to swing them though and they had to be held in both hands. This left the axe wielding soldier open to attack as he swung his weapon back.

Boom! Boom! Shake the room!

Gunpowder was used in China way back in the first century CE, but it wasn't until the fourteenth century that it came to Europe! At first, cannons – or 'thundertubes' – were as dangerous to the soldiers using them as they were to the enemy. Things did improve and even handguns started to appear on the battlefield by the fifteenth century. Although useful for scaring horses, guns and cannons didn't become really effective until the very end of the Middle Ages.

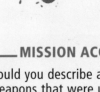

Work

1 Explain which two weapons you would choose if you were fighting a knight on horseback.

2 Why do you think guns weren't used more often on the medieval battlefield?

3 Draw a medieval man at arms or footsoldier carrying the weapons you would choose to take onto the battlefield (a maximum of three). Label your picture, clearly showing the names of the weapons and explaining why you have chosen them.

——— MISSION ACCOMPLISHED? ———

- Could you describe at least three different weapons that were used in the Middle Ages?
- Can you explain how they were used to kill people?
- Have you decided which weapon you would choose if you were on a battlefield in the Middle Ages?

British history could have been so different if King Edward IV hadn't overdone it one night in April 1483. The Yorkist King had eaten so much that he was forced to go to bed to sleep it off. He caught a fever there and never left his bed alive again! His 12-year-old son, Edward, was sent to London to be made king and was soon joined by his 10-year-old brother Richard. But Edward was never crowned and neither was his little brother. Both boys disappeared and their uncle became King Richard III. So what happened, and was foul play involved?

5: The Princes in the Tower

MISSION OBJECTIVES

- To understand why Edward V was never crowned king.
- To decide what happened to Edward and his brother and to explain the decision you have made.

EVIDENCE A

Written in 1483.
Prince Edward and his brother were taken to the inner rooms of the tower, and day by day began to be seen less behind the bars and the windows, until they stopped appearing altogether.

EVIDENCE B

A speech by a Frenchman in 1484.
Look at what has happened since the death of King Edward. His courageous children have been killed and the crown has gone to their murderer.

EVIDENCE C

Written in 'The Great Chronicle of London', 1512.
The children were seen shooting and playing in the garden until Easter [1484]. After Easter there was much whispering among the people that the king had put the children to death.

↵ **SOURCE A:** *This painting was created much later than the time the princes were alive. It is one artist's interpretation of how the princes might have looked.*

EVIDENCE D

Written in 1513 by Sir Thomas More. More was brought up by John Morton, a man who hated Richard III because he put him in prison in 1483.

King Richard wanted Sir James Tyrell to carry out his wishes. Tyrell decided that the princes should be murdered in their beds. He picked Miles Forest and John Dighton to do the job.

About midnight Forest and Dighton entered the room where the children lay in their beds and forced the feather bed and pillows hard into their mouths until they stopped breathing.

They laid their bodies out naked on the bed and fetched Sir James to see them. Then he got the murderers to bury them at the bottom of the stairs, deep in the ground under a heap of stones. Later a priest dug up the bodies and moved them to a place which only he knew.

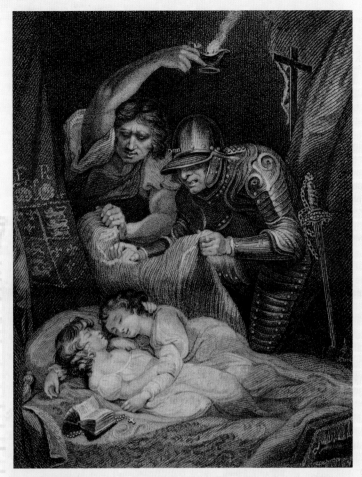

⤶ **SOURCE B:** *This painting is from the 20th century, and again is the artist's interpretation of what happened to the princes.*

EVIDENCE E

In 1674, some workmen were working on a staircase in the Tower of London. Two metres underground they discovered a box full of bones. The bones were reburied in Westminster Abbey. They are still there today.

EVIDENCE F

When the bones were discovered in 1674, Charles II, who was king at the time, placed them in a marble casket and gave them a full funeral. During the service, the Archbishop of London said this:
'It is right and meet that we commend the bones of these young princes to a place of final rest. Their fates at the order of Richard III grieves us, and though almost two centuries have passed, the vile deeds of that villain shall ne'er be forgotten.'

‖ PAUSE for Thought

Carbon dating is a technique scientists use to tell us how old something is. When the remains were examined in 1933 and 1955, carbon dating was not available to the scientists; they had to try and estimate how old things were by the way they looked. Do you think the bones should be re-examined so scientists can give us a much better idea of the age of the bones? How would this help us decide if the bones are indeed those of the Princes in the Tower?

EVIDENCE G

In 1933, two doctors examined the bones. Their report said:

- the skeletons were not complete;
- the bones belonged to two children aged about 10 and 12
- a stain on one of the skulls may mean that they could have been suffocated;
- the bones could have been there since 1100;
- the elder boy had a serious tooth disease.

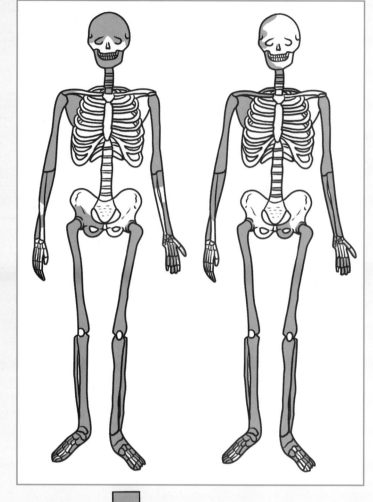

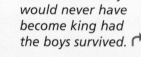 = *parts of the skeletons found*

EVIDENCE H

In 1955, other doctors looked at the report made in 1933. They weren't allowed to look at the bones but studied pictures instead. They said that:

- the bones were from children younger than the two princes;
- the stain was not caused by suffocation.

SOURCE C: *Henry VII would never have become king had the boys survived.* ↱

EVIDENCE I

By historian Phillip Lindsay in 1972.

Richard had no reason to kill them. Henry Tudor had every reason. Henry was capable of such a crime, so they were quietly murdered.

EVIDENCE J

There were many rumours at the time. Some said that the two boys had fallen off a bridge. Others said that Prince Edward had become ill and died naturally and that Prince Richard was secretly taken abroad.

↵ **SOURCE D:** *Richard III, the man who became king after the boys disappeared.*

EVIDENCE K

When Henry Tudor became king, he gave land and important jobs to James Tyrell, John Dighton and Miles Forest.

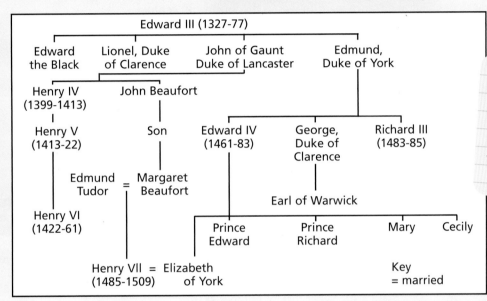

Edward III (1327-77)

Edward the Black — Lionel, Duke of Clarence — John of Gaunt Duke of Lancaster — Edmund, Duke of York

Henry IV (1399-1413) — John Beaufort

Henry V (1413-22) — Son — Edward IV (1461-83) — George, Duke of Clarence — Richard III (1483-85)

Edmund Tudor = Margaret Beaufort

Henry VI (1422-61)

Earl of Warwick

Prince Edward — Prince Richard — Mary — Cecily

Henry VII = Elizabeth
(1485-1509) of York

Key
= married

EVIDENCE L

This family tree shows how both Henry VII and Richard III benefited from the disappearance of the two princes.

Work

To try to solve this mystery, you need to look closely at all the evidence.

1 Find out about the events leading up to the disappearance of the two princes.

Think about where and when the princes were last seen. Why were they there?

2 Find a motive – who might want them dead and why?

Is there anybody who might benefit from the princes' deaths? Why are Richard III and Henry Tudor both suspects? Explain your ideas.

3 Find any evidence to show it might not have been a murder.

Perhaps the boys died of natural causes? Write down any ideas you have to support this theory.

4 Find any evidence for murder.

Is there any evidence to support the idea that the two princes were murdered? If so, how and by whom?

5 Consider whose evidence might not be reliable.

Could someone be making things up? Why might someone lie? Does any one piece of evidence contradict another? Write down your theories.

6 Now make your decision.

Write a short paragraph to explain what you think happened to the Princes in the Tower.

MISSION ACCOMPLISHED?

- Do you know why Edward V never made it to his coronation?
- Could you explain to somebody what you think happened to the Princes in the Tower?

Towards the end of the Middle Ages, England started to interfere in the affairs of neighbouring countries, in particular France. In fact, between 1337 and 1453, the English King also claimed he was the King of France! English armies invaded France and won famous victories in what became known as the Hundred Years' War. This marathon war gave both France and England some of their best known heroes and greatest victories in battle. Indeed, it was only after these wars that people in England thought of themselves as English. Beforehand, they were loyal only to their local baron or area.

1: Why was there a war that lasted for 100 years?

MISSION OBJECTIVES

- To know why England and France went to war in the fourteenth century.
- To understand why it became known as the Hundred Years' War.
- To know the chronological order of the battles that were fought.

In 1337 Edward III started a war with the French king, Philip VI. Neither of them was alive to see who had won when the fighting finally stopped. In fact, the wars were to last, with some long breaks in between, for the next 116 years. Historians chose to call this: The Hundred Years' War. So what were the two countries fighting about? What made these two countries fight for so long? And who finally came out on top?

1340
England win the Battle of Sluys. The English surprise the French ships while they are docked. Although the battle takes place at sea, it is fought by soldiers jumping from ship to ship who fight as if they are on land. The French defeat means England controls the Channel and can invade France whenever they feel like it.

1346
Edward enjoys another crushing victory on land. At the Battle of Crécy, his 12 000 archers and 2400 knights smashed 12 000 French knights, 6000 crossbowmen and 20 000 militiamen. The English archers had proven that they were far superior to the crossbowmen.

1347
Edward makes it a hat-trick of victories by capturing the French port of Calais. This is the closest port to England and was to remain in English hands for over 200 years.

1356
English victories continue at the Battle of Poitiers, led by Edward's son, The Black Prince. Philip VI was captured and held to ransom for £500 000. That's five times more than Edward normally earned in a year!

1370
The French start to fight back and, when the Black Prince falls ill, they win back some of their land.

Best of friends – worst of enemies!

The rulers of France and England had been linked since 1066. They shared the same ancestors and language, they traded with each other and they went to war in the Holy Land together. By the end of the Hundred Years' War, they were very different nations who were very suspicious of each other. When the French King Charles IV died without leaving behind any sons, the King of England, Edward III, claimed he should now be ruler of both nations. He was the nephew of Charles IV. The French weren't prepared to have an Englishman in charge and put Philip VI on their throne. Philip then further angered Edward by helping Scotland fight against England. The final straw came when Philip claimed that Edward's land in France, known as Aquitaine, was not rightfully Edward's. For Edward this could mean only one thing – war!

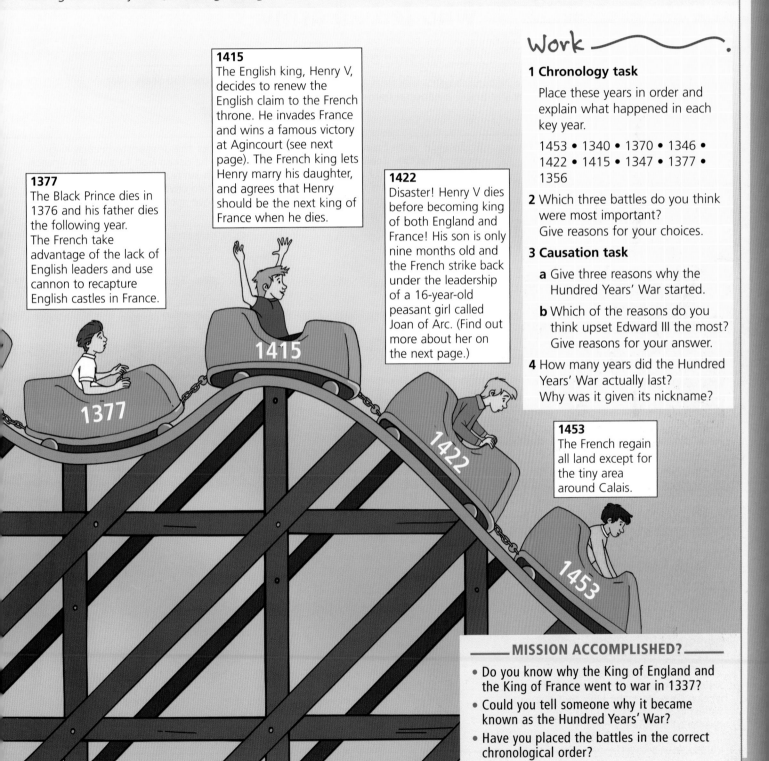

1415
The English king, Henry V, decides to renew the English claim to the French throne. He invades France and wins a famous victory at Agincourt (see next page). The French king lets Henry marry his daughter, and agrees that Henry should be the next king of France when he dies.

1377
The Black Prince dies in 1376 and his father dies the following year. The French take advantage of the lack of English leaders and use cannon to recapture English castles in France.

1422
Disaster! Henry V dies before becoming king of both England and France! His son is only nine months old and the French strike back under the leadership of a 16-year-old peasant girl called Joan of Arc. (Find out more about her on the next page.)

1453
The French regain all land except for the tiny area around Calais.

Work

1 Chronology task

Place these years in order and explain what happened in each key year.

1453 • 1340 • 1370 • 1346 • 1422 • 1415 • 1347 • 1377 • 1356

2 Which three battles do you think were most important? Give reasons for your choices.

3 Causation task

a Give three reasons why the Hundred Years' War started.

b Which of the reasons do you think upset Edward III the most? Give reasons for your answer.

4 How many years did the Hundred Years' War actually last? Why was it given its nickname?

──── MISSION ACCOMPLISHED? ────

- Do you know why the King of England and the King of France went to war in 1337?
- Could you tell someone why it became known as the Hundred Years' War?
- Have you placed the battles in the correct chronological order?

In the 1420s, England was on the verge of conquering all of France. But that all changed when a 16-year-old peasant girl went to see the French king and persuaded him to let her lead one his armies! So what on earth made the French put a schoolgirl in charge of an army? What made her such a good leader? And what happened to the greatest heroine in French history?

2: Joan of Arc – the teenage girl who led an army

MISSION OBJECTIVES

- To understand who Joan of Arc was and how she affected the outcome of the 100 Years' War.
- To understand why she is still a national hero in France today.

1: Joan was born in Domremy in 1412. At the age of 12, she claimed that Saint Catherine, Saint Margaret and Saint Michael 'visited' her and told her go to church. ▼

2: In 1428, with France on the verge of defeat, Joan claimed that the saints told her to go to the king and tell him to let her chase the English from France. ▼

3: Joan sees the desperate French king. She knows he asked God to save the French people from suffering. The king is amazed! He hadn't told anybody about his prayers – she must have spoken to God! ▼

▲ **4:** Joan is questioned about her visions by a panel of holy men for three weeks. They told the king that she was telling the truth and to put her in charge of one of his armies!

▲ **5:** Joan believes it was God's wish for her to go to Orleans, which was under seige by the English. She wore a suit of armour and immediately made the soldiers go to church, give up swearing and stop stealing. People said she was sent by God and men flocked to fight for her.

▲ **6:** Joan led an attack on the English. Despite being injured, she inspired the French to victory! Never again would the English control so much of France.

Joan of Arc's revenge!

Soon after her execution, people on both sides started to believe it was a mistake. Even while Joan was burning, an English onlooker is said to have cried out, 'We are lost, for we have burnt a saint.' The King of England's own secretary hurried back from the execution and said, 'We are all ruined, for a good and holy person was burned.' By 1453, England had lost all of its land in France apart from a tiny area around Calais.

↵ SOURCE A: *This statue of Joan of Arc is in the centre of Paris. She is still greatly admired by French people today.*

7: Joan continued to lead the French to victory in other battles. When the new French king was crowned, Joan stood next to him carrying her banner. ▼

8: Joan continued to fight the English but was betrayed and captured at the town of Compiegne. The French were devastated; the English were overjoyed! ▼

▲ **9:** Joan was put on trial for being a witch but there was not enough evidence. In the end, they decided that dressing as a man was enough proof of witchcraft and she was burned at the stake!

Work

1 Describe three ways in which Joan of Arc was different from the kind of people who usually led armies in the Middle Ages.

2 Why do you think so many people followed Joan into battle?

3 Why do you think that Joan of Arc is such a heroine in France today?

— **MISSION ACCOMPLISHED?** —

• Could you explain how Joan of Arc was different from people who usually led armies?

• Do you know how she helped the King of France?

• Do you know how Joan died and what happened to her after she died?

Of all the English kings that fought in the Hundred Years' War, Henry V came the closest to defeating the French. Within two years of becoming king, the 25-year-old had wiped out the best French leaders and generals. Within eight years he had been promised the French Crown when the old king died. Within nine years he was dead. So why was Henry V so successful at fighting the French? What weapons and tactics did he use to destroy the French knights at the Battle of Agincourt? And why is Agincourt such a famous battle in British history?

3: Why did the Battle of Agincourt make us stick two fingers up?

MISSION OBJECTIVES

- To understand why Henry V restarted the Hundred Years' War.
- To know how and why the English won the Battle of Agincourt.
- To decide why it was such a famous and important English victory.

Henry V decided to take advantage of a French civil war that was raging in 1415. He thought that, while the French were busy fighting each other, it would be easier to press home his claim to the throne. He attacked Harfleur and, after it surrendered, he marched north to Calais and then home. But the French had no intention of letting Henry get away. The English soldiers were outnumbered three to one, were exhausted and many were suffering from dysentry. They were desperate to get home but all hope seemed lost. On 25 October 1415, in a field near the village of Agincourt, the two sides squared up to each other. The field had recently been ploughed and the weather in the days leading up to the 25th had been heavy rain. These facts plus the dense woodland that surrounded the battlefield, would have a major impact on the outcome of the fighting.

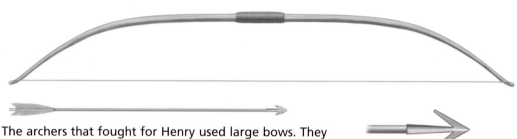

The archers that fought for Henry used large bows. They could fire ten arrows a minute and could kill a man at 180m. The bow had already proved it was a better weapon than the crossbow at the Battle of Crecy. The humble, common archer was about to prove he was a better soldier than a great and noble knight at the Battle of Agincourt.

Henry moved his archers to within range of the French knights and ordered them to open fire. The French tried to charge but a combination of thick mud, heavy armour and wooden spikes slowed them down. When the French did get through, they chose to attack the English knights instead of the archers. After all, it was far more impressive to kill a knight than a mere archer. The longbows were free to continue their long-range slaughter. At the end of the battle, thousands of French lay dead. English losses were only a few hundred men.

Après-Agincourt

After the massive victory at Agincourt, Henry conquered Normandy and tightened his grip on France. Many powerful French knights and nobles had been killed at Agincourt and, before long, the daughter of the French king had become Henry's wife. In 1420, the Treaty of Troyes was signed by the French king, Charles V. This was a contract that said that Henry was now the legal heir to the French throne.

Dysentry distress

Henry V never lived to be the king of both England and France – he died suddenly of dysentry in 1422 aged just 35. But his victories in France caused a huge surge in national pride and people were very proud to call themselves English. Henry V has remained one of England's greatest heroes.

SOURCE A: *Sir Lawrence Olivier played Henry V in extremely popular and successful film versions of Shakespeare's play. Olivier's version was made during World War II and was meant to make people proud of their country and support the war.* ↱

! FACT Punishing an archer
According to legend, the English archers terrified the French so much at Agincourt that they would have their first two fingers cut off when captured. That way, they could never draw back the deadly longbow again. To taunt the French, the English began sticking their fingers up at them. Rude people carry on the tradition to this day!

'We few, we happy few, we band of brothers;
For he to-day that sheds his blood with me
Shall be my brother; be he ne'er so vile,
This day shall gentle his condition;
And gentlemen in England now-a-bed
Shall think themselves accurs'd they were not here,
And hold their manhoods cheap whiles any speaks
That fought with us upon Saint Crispin's day.'

↰ **SOURCE B:** *This is part of the St Crispin's day speech from the Shakespeare play 'Henry V'. It was written over 200 years after the Battle of Agincourt, but it is one of the most famous things that Shakespeare ever wrote. This has helped to keep the memory and celebration of the victory alive amongst English people.*

Work

1 Why did Henry V think it was a good idea to invade France in 1415?

2 Some historians have described the longbow as the 'medieval machine gun'. Why do you think this is?

3 What problems were the English suffering from when the Battle of Agincourt started?

4 How did the weather help Henry win the battle?

5 Which weapon do you think was most important for Henry winning the battle? Give reasons for your answer.

6 What mistake did the French make when attacking the English?

7 Read Source A. How has Shakespeare helped keep Henry V a well-known and popular king?

—— **MISSION ACCOMPLISHED?**——

- Do you know why Henry V decided to invade France?
- Could you tell somebody which weapon helped Henry win the Battle of Agincourt?
- Do you know two reasons why the battle is so well known today?

SK 1 _____

ting from the bottom right-hand corner, this picture
ws an operation in the Middle Ages. Think about the
owing questions before writing a description of the
e in as much detail as you can.

What sort of operation is taking place?

What do you think is wrong with the patient?

Why is the doctor performing this operation?

What do you think happened to the patient?

Write down as many differences as you can see
between this operation and a modern-day operation.

TASK 2

Work out the following famous names from the Middle Ages by looking at the clues in brackets and filling in the missing consonants. Next to each name, write out the year (or years) they appear during the Middle Ages and then place the names in the correct chronological order.

_a_a_ _ _a_ _ _a_a (Norway's king)

_a_o_ _ _o_ _i_ _o_ (ouch my eye)

_i_ _i_ _ _ _e _o_ _ue_o_ (winner in 1066)

_ _o_a_ _e_ _e_ (friend and enemy of Henry II)

_oa_ o_ A_ _ (16 years old)

_a_ _ _ _e_ (peasant's leader)

_a_a_i_ (Saracen leader)

_e_ _ _ _u_o_ (winner in 1485)

_a_i_ _a (Stephen's cousin)

E_ _a_ _ (the Hammer of the Scots)

_i_ _ia_ _a_ _a_e (Braveheart)

_i_ _a_ _ _ _e _io_ _ea_ _ (famous crusader)

TASK 3

The sentences below don't make much sense. They need capital letters, commas, full stops and apostrophes.

a Copy the sentences, adding punctuation as you write.
  • the battles of stamford bridge and hastings were both in 1066
  • william the conqueror was king of england for 21 years
  • the best weapons to attack a castle were the siege tower the trebuchet and the battering ram
  • king henry always felt guilty about thomas beckets murder in canterbury cathedral
  • richard the lionhearts finest victory was at the battle of acre in 1191
  • king edwards nickname was the hammer of the scots
  • the black death was first reported in china and india in 1334
  • richard II was englands finest king
  • at the battle of agincourt in 1415 king henrys army defeated the French army easily
  • henry tudor became king after he defeated king richard in the battle of bosworth field

b In each sentence, underline the facts in blue and the opinions in red.

TASK 4

Apostrophes can be used to show possession (belonging). For example:
• The Revolt belonging to one peasant = The Peasant's Revolt.
  (In singular words, write the apostrophe before the 's'.)
• The Revolt belonging to two or more peasants = The Peasants' Revolt.
  (In plural words, the apostrophe is put after the 's'.)

1 Write out the following sentences, adding the apostrophe in the correct place at the end.
  a The ships belonging to William – Williams ships
  b Thomas was a friend of Henry – Henrys friend was Thomas
  c The land belonging to the barons – The barons land
  d The swords belonging to the soldiers – The soldiers swords
  e The huts belonging to the peasants – The peasants huts
  f The sun belonging to the king – The kings son

2 Are the following singular or plural? Write each one out, adding a 'p' or an 's' for plural or singular. One has been done for you.
  a King William's son = s
  b Peasant's Revolt
  c The baron's manor house
  d The knights' land
  e The monk's books
  f The monks' books
  g Richard's promises
  h The soldier's weapon
  i The king's castles
  j Rebels' punishment

TASK 5

Here are 12 groups of words phrases or names. In each group there is an odd-one-out. When you think you have found it, write a sentence or two to explain why you think it doesn't fit in with any of the others.

a Duke William • Harold Hardrada • King Edward • Harold Godwinson
b Normandy • Spain • England • Norway
c baron • motte • bailey • keep
d habit • sword • sandals • tonsure
e Thomas Becket • Richard Britto • Reginald Fitzurse • William de Traci
f archery • golf • football • baseball
f boils • bad breath • toothache • rash
h fire • murder • combat • water
i Agincourt • Poitiers • Jaffa • Crecy
j axe • shield • sword • crossbow

Glossary

Abbey A large monastery.

Advisors Men who helped the king decide what to do.

Afterlife Life after death.

Ale A watery kind of beer.

Anglo-Saxons Invaders from Germany who ruled from about 500 to 1066.

Archers Members of the army who used longbows to fire arrows at the enemy.

Astrolabe A tool developed by Muslims that could measure the distance between stars.

Bailey A large courtyard surrounded by a fence, part of a castle.

Barber-surgeon A medieval equivalent of a doctor.

Barbican A tower protecting the gate to a castle.

Bastide A town attached to a castle. It was for the English, even though it was in Wales.

Benefit of the clergy A way of being judged in a Church Court, if you could read a verse from the Bible.

Blood-letting The practice of making someone bleed to help cure an illness.

Borrow To take money from a moneylender which has to be paid back with interest.

Bubonic One of the two types of plague in the Black Death.

Chancellor An important job helping the king.

Charter A written agreement or set of promises.

Chivalry A special code of behaviour for knights.

Chronicles Diary of events.

Chronological order The order in which events happened, starting with the earliest.

Church This can mean one building or an entire Christian community, such as the Roman Catholic Church.

Church Court A court that was usually for priests, which gave lighter sentences.

Civil war War that takes place within a country between two different groups.

clans A Scottish tribe.

commoners In the Middle Ages, knights who were in the House of Commons.

Commons Representatives of ordinary people in Parliament.

Concentric castle A type of medieval castle with rounded towers and different height walls, that was easier to defend.

Conqueror The name by which King William I is known, having successfully invaded England and become king.

Consecrated Made holy, in a special ceremony.

Constable A man in charge of a group of watchmen.

Daub Mud, dung and straw, smeared over wattle to make a wall.

Disbanded Broken up as a group.

Discipline Keeping people in order.

Disease Illness or sickness, usually caused by infection.

Disembowelled To cut open someone's stomach and pull out their insides, used as a punishment.

Doom paintings Paintings in church to remind the people about heaven and hell.

Dowry Money or gifts given to a husband by his wife's family after marriage.

Dysentery A disease which causes terrible diarrhoea.

Earldom An area of land that an earl looks after.

Evidence Information that helps a person to form an opinion.

Excommunicated This is when someone is banned from going to church – a terrible punishment in the

Middle Ages as it meant you would go to hell when you died.

Feudal system A system of dividing up land; men received land in return for offering to fight or provide a service for their lord.

Flagellants People who whipped themselves in order to ask God to forgive them for their sins.

Franks The word used by Saracens to describe the Crusaders.

Freeman A person who is free from his duties to his lord.

Fyrd King Harold's ordinary soldiers.

Garderobes Medieval toilets.

Guild A club or society of traders and merchants.

Germs The cause of disease.

Hauberks Long coats of chain mail.

Heir Next in line to be king or queen.

Hermit A man who lives on his own and has no contact with anybody.

Highlands The mountain area of Scotland.

Homage A promise of loyalty to the king.

Housecarls One of King Harold's best soldiers.

Houses The two parts of Parliament, made up of the Lords and the Commons.

Hue and cry A noisy group of people who chased criminals.

Illuminated Capital letters decorated by monks in their books.

Individually Acting on your own.

Inferior Of poor quality.

Insanity Madness.

Intolerance Lack of respect for people who are different in some way.

Isolated Left in a dangerous position, without enough help.

Jury A group of people who decide if a person is guilty or innocent of a crime.

Keep The strongest part of a castle.

Knights Men who promise to fight for their lord.

Lance A weapon; a long spear usually tipped with steel.

Latin An Ancient Roman language, still popular in the Middle Ages.

Leeches Blood-sucking creatures used in medieval medicine.

Lend Give money to some for a while, which they had to give back with interest. In the Middle Ages, Jews were moneylenders.

Looting Stealing.

Lords of the marches The barons who were given land on the Welsh borders by William the Conqueror.

Loyalty Faithfulness; if a person promised loyalty, they promised to support someone.

Mace A club with a spiked metal head.

Manuscripts Books written by hand by monks.

Massacred A large number of people being killed.

Miracle play A medieval play based on a story from the Bible or about a saint.

Mitre An abbot's headdress.

Monastery A building where monks live.

Monk Man who dedicate his life to worshipping God.

Motte A large mound of earth on which a keep is usually built.

Negotiate To talk until you reach agreement.

Norman A man from Normandy, an area of France.

Ordeal A medieval way of finding out if a person was guilty of a crime or not.

Page A young boy training to be a knight.

Parchment Animal skin treated to form a sort of paper for books.

Pardons Special letters that forgive a person for a crime.

Parliament The body of Lords and Commons set up to rule the country with the King.

Patriotic Loyal to your own country.

Paying homage Knights fighting 40 days for the king in return for land.

Pilgrim A person who makes a journey to a holy place.

Pilgrimage A religious journey.

Pillory A wooden frame with holes for head and hands, used as a punishment.

Pneumonic One of the two types of plague in the Black Death.

Poll tax A tax that everyone pays; people all paid the same amount no matter what they could afford.

Pope The leader of the Roman Catholic Church.

Power struggles When different people compete to have the most power.

Relics The ancient remains of a person or animal.

Retreating An army that is retreating is going back because they realise they can't win the battle.

Revolt Another word for a rebellion or uprising.

Rosary A string of beads using in praying.

Rye bread A dark, heavy bread made of rye, not wheat.

Saint A person who, after they have died, is considered by the Church to be especially good.

Sanctuary A safe place, such as a church.

Saracens The word used by the Crusaders to describe Muslims.

Scavengers A person or animal who lives off the things other people have thrown away.

Scold's bridle A head brace used to punish a nagging wife, sometimes called a Scold's brace.

Scriptorium A writing room in a monastery.

Shield-wall A long line of shields in a battle.

Shrine A holy place visited by pilgrims, often the tomb of a saint.

Spears Long pointed weapons.

Stocks A wooden frame with holes for feet, used as a punishment.

Sultan The ruler of a Muslim country.

Symptoms Signs of illness or disease.

Tithe A tax that people had to pay to the local priest, usually one tenth of their farm produce.

Tithings A group of 10 people who were responsible for each other's behaviour.

Treasurer The man who looked after the king's money.

Trenchers Slices of stale bread used as plates.

Trepanning Drilling a hole in a patient's head in the belief that this would cure their headache.

Tudor Rose The emblem created by Henry Tudor that is a mixture of the white York rose and the red Lancaster rose.

Vikings Invader from Denmark, Sweden or Norway.

Villein Peasant.

Wandering minstrel A man who travelled round the country singing songs to people. He was often able to tell the people what was happening in the country.

Watch A group of people who patrolled the streets at night.

Wattle Sticks woven together.

Witan Before the Normans arrived in England, this was a group of the most important bishops and earls.

Work Service A system in which peasants had to work

Index